Authentic
Arabian Horse Names

Authentic

Arabian Horse Names

A Collection of Arabic Names
with Translations and Pronunciations
Especially for the Arabian Horse Lover

By Bachir Bserani
with Kellie Kolodziejczyk

Printed in the United States of America by
Josten's Printing and Publishing, Topeka, Kansas

ISBN# 0-9763022-0-9

Design and Production:Kellie Kolodziejczyk, Bachir Bserani and Joe Ferriss
Arabic Calligraphy by Bachir Bserani
Graphics by JF Graphics

Published by, Al Moussami, LLC
PO Box 566, Central Square, NY 13036
Website: www.al-moussami.com

Front Cover: *When Bargaining Gets Tight,*
painting by Andre Pater, Polish/American, b. 1953. Painted 1986
Front and Back Cover Design: Joe Ferriss
Endsheets: *Gaët Shammar Moving Their Camp,* nineteenth century engraving,
reprinted from Lady Anne Blunt, *The Bedouins of the Euphrates,* (1879) opp. 188,
courtesy of the Joe Ferriss collection

Contents

Acknowledgements

I owe a debt of gratitude to those who,

during the years, gracefully accepted

to listen to my stories and

share my knowledge of horses.

Over the years, there were many people

who have contributed to the development of this book.

I learned a lot from my students and their horses,

from my teachers and their theories,

but most of all, my true knowledge

comes from the desert;

the harsh environment which helped

mold the Arabian horse

as the world's most beautiful

and admired breed of horse.

Bachir Bserani

"If you have seen nothing
but the beauty of their markings
and limbs, their true beauty
is hidden from you."
—Al Moutanabi

About the Authors

For as long as he can remember, Bachir Bserani, a native to the Middle Eastern country of Syria, has loved and admired the beautiful and exotic Arabian horse. Arabian horses have always been a part of his life, and the Middle Eastern culture in which he was raised. Childhood memories remain vivid as Bachir recalls his first experiences with these magnificent horses. Often he and his father would ride together, through the Syrian Desert, upon a most elegant chestnut Arabian mare. Her name was *Al Mounjer,* meaning *The Fortune Teller,* in the Arabic language. These outings were wonderfully joyful and exciting as, during their travel, Bachir and his father would stop to visit with the Bedouin tribes, and listen to their mystifying stories and legends of the desert. Bachir particularly enjoyed learning the Bedouin techniques with respect to riding, caring for, naming, and even talking to their horses with the soft, soothing melody of their voices.

Al Mousssami, *The Man Who Names the Horses.*

Left Bachir Bserani

Left Few photos remain from Bachir Bserani's earlier days in the Middle East. Although poor in quality, this photo shows Bachir Bserani standing (to the left) with his Saklawi-Kuhaylan stallion, *Amir.*

Despite the tragic death of his father when Bachir was still very young, his passion and desire for the horses remained strong. After attending classes at his school each day, Bachir could always be found riding and tending to the horses at the nearby stable. But, it wasn't until he graduated from school that Bachir acquired his very own Arabian horse. A most generous gift from his mother, the beautiful *Saklawiyah* strain mare, named *Rheemah,* was Bachir's most cherished possession. Within a few years Bachir was able to purchase several more outstanding Arabians including a stallion named *Sultan,* a mare named *Aroussah,* a stallion named *Lateef,* and a *Saklawi-Kuhaylan* stallion named *Amir.*

Bachir took great pride in all of his Arabian horses. It was *Rheemah,* however, who was most dear to his heart, for her beauty and speed were unparalled. After winning countless races in the desert with her, Bachir attracted the attention of many, including the well respected Colonel Posselle, a former instructor/trainer of the famous Spanish Riding School. In Syria at the request of the government, the Colonel was summoned to instruct the government's mounted Cavalry on riding, jumping, and for the schooling of the Cavalry horses as well. Having been impressed by Bachir's riding abilities and dedication towards the Arabian horse, the Colonel encouraged the young equestrian to become his apprentice. Without hesitation, the proposal was accepted. For the next several years Bachir studied

Dressage and, under the Colonel's direction, learned advanced riding and training techniques. Later, Bachir went on to join the Syrian Riding Team, attending competitions throughout the Middle East and Europe. During this period, he also had the opportunity to attend *La Federation du Club Hippique au Liban*, an Equestrian school in Beirut, Lebanon, where he earned a Certificate of Merit as an Equestrian Professor, Trainer, and International Rider.

Then, at nearly 30 years old and in the prime of his life, Bachir suddenly made the decision to leave the Middle East to come to the United States. He settled in the state of Texas where he opened Abbey Downs Riding School, a facility dedicated to the education of horse and rider. Inevitably, Bachir became widely known to the American Arabian horse community. He was highly sought after by owners and breeders not only for his knowledge of horses, but also, for his knowledge of the Middle Eastern culture and language. In the early 1980's, responding to a need for guidance on how to properly name Arabian foals, Bachir published the booklet, *What Is My Name?*, a collection of authentic Arabic names for Arabian horses. The booklet was a huge hit with Arabian horse enthusiasts, and helped to generate a greater understanding and awareness of *appropriate* Arabic names for Arabian horses. Bachir continued to operate his stable, Abbey Downs Riding School, for over a decade before retiring and relocating, along with his two daughters Chantal and Nicole, to Upstate New York.

Right This photo was taken in Syria just before Bachir Bserani left to come to the United States. It shows Bachir mounted upon his Kuhaylan stallion, *Lateef,* and with a few of his fellow horsemen.

Right Bachir Bserani, in competition, with one of his prized Arabian horses.

Not only an accomplished horseman, but also an accomplished scholar, Bachir is fluent in Arabic, French, and the English languages. After moving to New York State, he earned his degree in Education, and began teaching high school level French language class. Since then, Bachir's days have become busier than ever. When not teaching his high school classes, he gives private riding instruction, schools horses, and continues to advise horse owners and breeders, forever dedicated to his passion for horses. Bachir Bserani resides near Syracuse, New York.

Kellie Kolodziejczyk, a personal friend and also a client of Bachir Bserani, was immediately intrigued by his stories and knowledge about Arabian horses, as well as his Middle Eastern heritage. Knowing Bachir's desire to share his vast knowledge and experiences with others, Kellie collaborated with Bachir to publish this newly revised and expanded collection of Arabian horse names. An avid animal lover, Kellie shares Bachir's respect and admiration for the Arabian horse. She, along with her husband Perry, breed and raise purebred Arabian and Pintabian horses. Their farm Abmor Acres, is located in Pennellville, New York.

Right Co-Author, Kellie Kolodziejczyk

Arabian mares of the Hamdani Ibn Ghorab family with the Shammar Bedouin tribe, 1996.
photo © Joe Ferriss

Foreword

I have never forgotten the elation I felt upon the discovery of the Arab horse over three decades ago. It is as though it was only yesterday. In my experience, the Arab horse touches the heart of one so deeply perhaps because it retains the essence of the gazelle and other free born wildlife while being a most loyal companion as well as a trustworthy, intelligent and enduring mount. The character of the Arab horse is almost indescribable yet it has, for centuries, been the inspiration of many Bedouin poets.

The Arab horse is undeniably a product of the Bedouin culture, having refined it into a unique equine that embodies all we admire in nature and in human interaction. Like their native American tribal counterparts in North America, the Bedouin have lived a life interwoven and dependent on harmony with nature. The Arabian horse bears testament to the quality of horse needed for the Bedouin lifestyle in harsh desert conditions.

When we become entrusted with the care and raising of Arabians it is only natural that we consider celebrating the roots that created this fine steed by drawing upon the legend, poetry and language of the tribes that have given us this legacy.

The real pleasure in this book is that it brings together the enthusiasm and style of a young American benefactor of the Arab horse, Kellie Kolodziejczyk, and the inherent knowledge of a seasoned horseman born of the Arab culture, Bachir Bserani, originally from the region of the few remaining Bedouin horse breeding tribes, which I personally have had the good fortune to visit. This is a book that offers, in an artful way, a window into the Bedouin's tent—to share in the delight of legend, the joy of naming a newborn foal, and the personal pride of maintaining the centuries old tradition of gracing the Arab horse with its deserving Arab name.

—Joe Ferriss

The True Naming
of the
Arabian Horse

The Bedouin people

customarily

congratulated each other

on three occasions:

The birth of a son,

the emergence

of a poet within a tribe,

and

when a foal was born.

The main purpose of this publication is to assist Arabian, and part Arabian horse owners with selecting proper and true Arabic names for their foals. It is a wonderful privilege to own one of these majestic horses. I hope that you will agree as you read through these pages that naming the Arabian foal is an important process that requires thoughtful care and consideration if we are to honor the Arabian horses of today, as they have been honored for centuries past.

Upon the first creation of the horse, according to ancient Bedouin legend, God presented the Bedouins with a beautiful and noble creature. And God spoke,

"...I create you, Arabian, and you are the most
Blessed of all the animals. Wealth will be carried
on your back and kindness in your eyes.
Bedouins, let your horses
run freely, feed them from the green fields and
meadows, and let your horses drink from your well.
If you do this, then you will be rewarded on
judgement day."

The Arabian horse is believed to have originated centuries ago in ancient Arabia, along the fertile Tigris and Euphrates Rivers. The people of the desert, or Bedouins, as they are called, revered these beautiful and celestial horses. Their admiration and devotion to the Arabian horse was woven into their culture and religion. Followers of Islam, the Bedouins deeply respected the teachings of the Prophet Mohammed and The Holy Koran. It is written in The Koran about the horse, and the Prophet, who greatly admired the horse, often spoke of them in his teachings to the Bedouins.

Traditionally, the desert Bedouins named their foals according to their color, markings, temperament, courage, and personality, as well as other similar traits. It was fabled about the Prophet that he owned a mare called *Al Awrah*, *The One-Eyed Mare*, so named because she was blinded in one eye. According to the legend, this mare had saved the Prophet in a battle, from where he was surrounded by the enemy. With great courage and strength *Al Awrah* fled with the Prophet, saving him from certain death. The Prophet was always kind to the horse. He taught the Bedouins to respect their horses, and to treat them as well as they treat their children.

The Bedouin people embraced and loved the horse very much. In fact, they customarily congratulated each other on three occasions: the birth of a son, the emergence of a poet within a tribe, and when a foal was born. These three happenings were the most highly regarded happenings in a Bedouin's life. You see, to the Bedouins, the Arabian signified wealth, social status and religious beliefs. They bred their horses with deliberate care, devoted to keeping them pure, or *Asil*, in the form intended by God. With its many unique characteristics, including the beautiful high neck and tail carriage, elegantly dished head with beautiful large eyes set widely apart, flaring nostrils, light prancing gait, and loving temperament, the Arabian epitomized strength, courage, pride, and unwavering loyalty. Furthermore, the Bedouins believed the bulging forehead of the Arabian horse, called the *Jabha* in Arabic, held the many blessings bestowed by *Allah*, or God. This Divine gift from *Allah* was to be treasured and nurtured. Arabian horses accompanied the Bedouins in almost every aspect of their lives. They carried their masters on their backs in battle, and even took shelter with their masters in their tents.

Over time, as generations of Arabian horses were born and raised, particular families, or strains, of Arabians emerged. The dominant strains were the *Hamdani*, *Obeyan*, *Kuhaylan*, *Saklawi*, and *Hadban*, each named after the tribe that bred them. The Bedouins believed,

The beautiful half-Arabian foal Al Moulawan with his dam Nadira.

*Traditionally, the desert Bedouins
named their foals
according to their color, markings,
temperament, courage, and personality.*

however, that the five families were born of five mares, the most beloved and loyal mares of the Prophet Mohammed. In the Arabic language, the Arabian horse strains are referred to as *Al Khamse* meaning, *The Five Ones*.

The Arabian strains varied slightly in type, size, and conformation. The *Hamdani* strain, known for their racing ability, were large boned, athletic type horses. The *Obeyan* strain, often shown off by the tribesmen, were quite refined, with slightly longer than average backs. The *Kuhaylan* strain, endowed with broad chests and muscular build, were accomplished endurance horses. The *Saklawi* strain were very feminine in appearance, with fine bones, chiseled features and exotic beauty. The *Hadban* strain were smaller, yet well-muscled, working-type horses. In these early days no written records were kept, however, the ancient legends describe how the Bedouins could accurately recant the pedigrees of their horses for many past generations.

For centuries the Arabian horse remained isolated, however, with the advent of exploration, these horses of the desert inevitably became known to the outside world. As word spread of the majestic horses of the desert, they were very much sought after. Many fine Arabian mares and stallions were taken back to the foreign lands, and bred with the native horses, adding the wonderful qualities of the Arabian to their existing herds. In time, so cherished were they, that many private and government-run Arabian horse breeding farms were established. Additionally, Arabian horse bloodlines were used in the development and refinement of many other breeds, most notably the Thoroughbred. As respect and admiration for the Arabian horse continued to grow, so, too, did the number of Arabian horses worldwide.

This love and devotion to the Arabian horse is still very strong today. Like the Bedouins, our relationship with our Arabians is far beyond an animal that we ride or feed. They are a part of us, of who we are. I too, have had the wonderful experience, and privilege, of owning Arabian horses. Born in the Middle Eastern country of Syria, I was always in the company of Arabian horses. They were a part of our family, life, and culture. When one is raised in the Middle East, you are taught to appreciate the Blessed gift of the Arabian horse. My love for horses was born into me, but also, I learned from my father, whom I looked up to very much. I would watch, and help him groom, wash, care for, and talk to his horse. I soon realized what a good companion the Arabian was. I saw, too, how they appreciate what we do for them. My mother would pretend to complain to me that I spent more time in the barn than at home, but she always understood my attraction to the horses. At times, she would watch me with a tear in her eye. As my father died at an early age, I think, maybe, she saw my father reflected in me.

My mother always encouraged my passion for the horses. The first Arabian horse I ever owned, I will never forget her, was a beautiful dapple-gray *Saklawiyah* mare named *Rheemah*. In Arabic, *Rheemah* means *Morning Dew*. She was the most special horse to me. I think I spent more time hugging her, and brushing her, than riding her. I had wanted this mare so very much, like I had never wanted anything else before. I will tell you the story of her.

I was about eighteen years old when I had first heard about *Rheemah*. A friend spoke to me of a beautiful *Saklawiyah* strain mare that was for sale in the desert. She was said to be purely exquisite. It was rumored that the owner was a wise, old, Bedouin that was no longer able to care for her, but that he had turned away many buyers, because he did not believe they would give her the home he wanted for her. After hearing this, I hurried home to tell my mother about the beautiful mare in the desert. She said that, as a gift for finishing my schooling, she would give me the money to purchase the mare, but that it was up to me to convince the Bedouin to sell me the horse.

I became very excited about the prospect of owning such a beautiful creature. I took my friend, and we traveled the five hours from

Damascus to the town of Hama where the Bedouin's tribe was. When we reached the village, we asked about the old man and his horse. The villagers pointed out his tent to us. It seemed like an eternity, but, at last, we reached the tent. The entranceway was open. Without entering, I called out loudly, "Is it you, Sir, who owns a *Saklawiyah?*" The old man, whom we had learned was named *Abou Mahmood,* came to the entranceway, and motioned for us to come inside. He said, "Yes, I have a *Saklawiyah.* She is three years old."

The old man was very weak and frail. I introduced my friend and myself to him, and gently shook his hand. I then asked if it was his *Saklawiyah* that was said to be for sale. The Bedouin looked at me in a peculiar way, and responded after a brief pause, "Well, now son, that all depends."

As I had heard the rumors about this old, wise man, I knew I had to prove myself worthy to own his prized horse. *Abou Mahmood* wanted to know everything about me. I told him my name, about my parents and family, where I came from, about my life, and my experiences with horses. The old man was gently nodding with his head as I spoke, listening very carefully to every word I said. When I was done, he looked up at me, and then asked if I would like to see his horse. I was so surprised, and filled with anticipation. I think he could sense my excitement since, before I could even respond, *Abou Mahmood* had put his arm around me, and was taking me to the next tent over.

When we entered the tent I could see, standing in front of us, the most beautiful horse I, truly, had ever seen. She was a blue-gray color with the most pretty head. Her large, kind eyes were looking right at us. I could see that this mare was something special. The old man asked us to sit. He poured us some tea, and then lowered himself to sit, ever so slowly. With a deep sigh, he began to tell us what this mare meant to him. He said, "I owned the grandmother of this mare.

I have lost all of my horses through age, and this is the one I have left. I come here every morning to drink my tea, and I talk to my beloved *Rheemah*. Many people think that I am senile because I am eighty years old, but she talks back to me. And this, I say, is what makes me live." I then asked *Abou Mahmood*, "But, why must you sell her?" He responded, "I am no longer able to care for her. My children have all moved on to other places. I only want for her to go to a good house." "*I* will give her a good house." I interrupted. "This I, most honorably, promise to you."

Abou Mahmood smiled and continued on. "I know you come from a good family and where you will take her. You are good to your horses. This is all that matters. I want you to take the best care of her." I assured the old man, once again, that I would. Much time passed, as we continued to sit for a while, talking about the horses. Then, *Abou Mahmood* said to me, "Bachir, I will sell you the horse." I thought that, surely, my ears were deceiving me.

I gave *Abou Mahmood* the money as he came near to me to shake my hand, and give me the Bill of Sale. Slowly, he then moved toward the mare, and took the lead rope that was draped over her back, putting it in my hands. As he did this, the old man's eyes filled with tears. I could see that he did not want to let her go. Graciously, I thanked *Abou Mahmood*, took the mare, and then led her away with the sun shining brightly on her magnificent coat. Never had I seen a horse in such perfect condition. As we walked towards the truck, the mare was prancing around a bit. I think she was uneasy about leaving her master, for when we were nearly to the truck, *Rheemah* pulled away with all her strength. Despite my efforts, I could not hold onto her. As swiftly as the wind, she galloped back to the tent where she had been, and to the old man.

My friend and I chased as fast as we could after the horse. As we were running back towards the tent we could see *Abou Mahmood* standing there, alone, outside the tent, with his long robe, long beard, and with worry beads in his hands. Worry beads to the Muslims are similar to what the rosary is to the Catholic religion, a medium for prayer. The horse I did not see. When we reached the tent, *Abou Mahmood* asked plainly, "Can I help you gentlemen?" as though, never before, had he met us.

I said, "Yes sir, I am coming back for my horse." And the old Bedouin, looking directly into my eyes, asked, "What horse?" Out of breath and confused, I looked at my friend, and then, to *Abou Mahmood*. Softly, I spoke, "The horse I just bought from you." I pulled out of my pocket the Bill of Sale to show him. Maintaining his stare, the old man calmly said to me, "Son, you did not buy any horse from me."

When I looked back into the eyes of the old man, I began to realize that I must have done something terribly wrong. I turned to my friend and said, "Let us go. I do not own that horse." And I began to walk away.

My friend wanted to persist, but I urged him to leave with me. As we were walking away *Abou Mahmood* called out my name. I turned to him, and as I did, he said, "Son, you forgot your horse." And there stood the old man with *Rheemah*.

Now, it really was a puzzle in my mind. I did not know what this meant. "*Is* he senile?" I thought to myself. As I stood there not able to move, the old man, again, said, "Son, you have forgotten your horse. Do you not want her back?" I did go back to get her, but before *Abou Mahmood* handed the mare over to me he said, "Son, you must learn something in life. By law, *Rheemah* is my horse because the law in the desert says, if you buy a horse, and it gets loose from you, and it returns to its previous owner, then you do not own the horse. But because you are new to this, and you are a young man needing to learn, I am going to give you the horse. But always remember this. If you have something as beautiful as this mare, never let it go." So, my friend and I took the horse with both of us holding the rope ever so tightly. We put *Rheemah* on the truck and went. And never again did I see the old, and very wise, *Abou Mahmood*.

I really loved showing off *Rheemah* to all my friends and neighbors back at home. I particularly enjoyed showing her off at the races. She was so fast. Many of the horsemen in Damascus belonged to the racing club. On Fridays, we would meet in the desert and prepare to race. We would dress up our horses beautifully with feathers and *panache*, and our best desert saddles. *Panache* is a French word for the costumes which adorned the horses. We always had blue in the cloth and blue beads, as the Arabic people believe the color blue wards off evil. The men and boys dressed up as Bedouins in the traditional garb. We were reenacting, for fun, how the Bedouins of the old time would race their horses in the desert. It was a joyous public gathering with music and dancing.

The race was very simple. We would race in the desert one half-mile; turn around at the white flag, and race back to the finish one-half mile. The winner would receive a lamb, or something like this, as a prize. Like the Bedouins, we were proud of our horses, and of their quality, athletic ability, and beauty. This was a celebration of our heritage. And really, *Rheemah* was one of the best horses I ever owned. At times, I just wanted to look at, and admire her. She was so beautiful. In the mornings I would turn her out, and it was, almost, as though, somebody had told her how beautiful she was, and she understood. With her prancing, running, and playing, she always showed off how pretty she was.

I think we all might have special stories of endeared horses in our lives. Much good as well as some misfortune happened to me over the next several years which led me to make the difficult decision to

You will see in this publication the Arabic names that I have chosen personally. I could have chosen to list thousands of words as in standard Arabic dictionaries, however, I chose to select only authentic Arabian horse names from various Arabic dialects including Syrian, Jordanian, Lebanese, and Egyptian that are the most easily pronounced by those who do not speak Arabic, and then put them in their masculine and feminine forms, with each name listed as appropriate for either a colt or a filly. But something must first be understood about the Arabic language. There are certain letters and syllables in the Arabic alphabet that English and other Romantic Language speaking people cannot easily pronounce. For example, *My Heart* written in Arabic is *Ya Kalbee*. I cannot write this with English lettering, so that you would pronounce it properly in Arabic, to keep the meaning *My Heart*. For you to pronounce it in Arabic the way it is written in English lettering would mean *My Dog*. As with the name *Ya Kalbee*, a similar situation occurs with the name *To Stay With Me Forever* which in the Lebanese dialect is *Dayimeh Maii,* whereby I cannot give an exact English lettering equivalent to the sound of the Arabic letter ﻉ which is made in the pronunciation of *Maii*. In Egyptian, however, *To Stay With Me Forever* is *Dayimah Wayayah*. This is a true desert name for an Arabian horse, is very easily pronounced, and was therefore included in this book. Beside every Arabic name listed I have included the authentic Arabic lettering, the English translation, and also the phonetic pronunciation to further assist you with properly speaking the word to keep the meaning as intended.

As you spend time watching your precious foals grow and develop their own unique personalities and traits, it is hoped that this publication will be useful in, not only, choosing just the perfect Arabic name for your youngster, but also, in understanding the nature of these special creatures. Not only when you are trying to select a name for your horse, but every day, look at your horse, listen to your horse and truly feel your horse. That little nicker they make may be their way of expressing how happy they are to see you. Now you, proud Arabian horse owners, can introduce your horse with *true* desert Arabian names. *Mabrouk!* Congratulations!

Bachir Bserani
with Kellie Kolodziejczyk

Hikayat Al Khayyal
The Story of the Horseman

Even today,

if one travels to the Middle East,

there are places in the desert

where there is found

Al Hakawati, The Storyteller.

And fantastic stories

can be heard about the desert

and its people,

ancient traditions and customs, and

especially myths and lore

about the beautiful and mystical

Arabian Horse.

In the old time there once lived a King in the Saudi Desert whose love for horses was so well known, that people would come from near and far to bestow the gift of the Arabian horse upon him. Having a keen eye for the Divine qualities and beauty of the Arabian horse, the King accepted only the finest mares and stallions into his stable.

One day the King called for his messengers, and he told them, "I want two horses. I want two of the finest horses to ever enter my stable. This will be a gift to my newborn son, Amir Al Sahra, The Great Prince of the Desert. And so, the messengers departed right away on their journey. They traveled many miles into the desert, spreading the word to the Bedouins of the wish of the King.

The Bedouins sent the most heavenly and beloved horses they possessed. The horses were carefully groomed, and then beautifully decorated with elegant halters and saddles, that were exquisitely detailed with colorful feathers, and finely woven cloth. Upon the horses mounted each tribe's most talented moudareb, or horse handler, plainly dressed, so as not to distract the King's eye from the beauty of the horse.

Many days and nights passed as the King anxiously awaited the return of his messengers, until, one day, the messengers returned with many horses. And the horses, as the King looked upon them, were more beautiful than he could ever have imagined. The King, being shaded under a large tent among his advisors, asked for the horse handlers to line up their horses in front of him, so he could decide which of them he would choose.

The first moudareb to approach stood his horse proudly before the King. The finely boned chestnut mare stood tall, with her delicately arching neck, and pretty head, turned toward the King; her large, round eyes looking kindly upon him. The King, seemingly drawn by her hypnotic gaze, walked toward the mare.

As he approached, the mare gently lowered her head to the King, as though she wanted him to receive the many blessings that she carried with her in the great bulge of her jabha. The King placed his hand upon her forehead, and then gently brushed his hand down the deep, concave arc of her face, to her small, refined muzzle. She is, indeed, thought the King, one of God's most perfect creatures.

To come next, before the King, was a well-muscled, dark bay stallion. Despite his great size, the stallion moved with a cadence and grace rarely ever seen. The majestic bay, with his supple carriage, danced rhythmically before the King, lifting his legs, one at a time, to the steady beat of the drums. His knees and hocks rose high to the heavens, and the stallion would float in the air for a moment in time, before starting his dance over, again and again.

And each moudareb, as he brought his horse before the King, did all he could to let the King choose his horse, because he knew there would be great reward to follow. The King watched carefully, each horse, but could not decide which of them he wanted. They were all of excellent breed, and beautiful. The King, through one of his advisors, then asked every horse handler, "What age is his horse?" But, not one of the horse handlers knew the age of the horse.

The King, then loudly proclaimed, "I want two of these fine horses, no more. But I want a young one, never reached beyond the age of 3, and I want an older one, one that has reached beyond the age of 15. Is there no one here in this crowd who can tell the age of a horse?"

The advisor of the King pointed out to the crowd, and said, "There is the one, Al Khayyal, The Horseman, whom I have heard rumors can tell the age of a horse." So the King sent for him. And the horseman, very old, and nearly bent in two, walking with a cane, slowly came toward the King, guided by a young boy.

"Greetings, King." said the horseman. "You call upon me, Sir?"

The King said to the horseman, "I do. Your King is here with a choice he is not able to make. Here before me are 20 of the most cherished of God's creatures. They are all of excellent breed, and beautiful. But, I want only two of them, a young one never reached beyond the age of 3 years old, and I want an older one, that went beyond the age of 15. Can you help me, horseman?"

The horseman responded, "Yes, I can help you Al Sharif, The Most Noble One, but you must know…I am a blind man."

The King asked, "You cannot see? But my advisors have told to me you know how to pick the horses."

The horseman responded, "Yes King, if you will allow me, I will pick the two horses for you."

The crowd was silent. Everyone was thinking how is this man, who is blind, able to pick a young horse and an older horse from a number of 20 horses. So the horseman asked one favor of the King. He said,

"I have my young grandson here with me. Would you allow him to guide me to the water?"

And the King, wanting to see how the old man was to pick the horses replied, "Yes, of course, horseman. Anything you desire, and it is done.

Once at the water, the horseman called for each horse handler to bring his horse to the water to drink. And, one by one, the horse handlers brought their horse to the water. Of course, all the horses being on a long journey from the desert were thirsty, and started to drink. The horseman stood very silent, and still. Not even did he touch the horses.

When all the horses had a chance to drink, the horseman announced to the King that the horses he wants are the fifth horse, and the twelfth horse. The horseman said, "The fifth horse has not reached beyond the age of 3 years old, and the twelfth horse has reached beyond the age of 15." And so, the King declared he would take the fifth horse, and the twelfth horse for the newborn Prince.

Now the King was fascinated to know how this old horseman, who was blind, knew the age of the horses. The horseman said, "It is very simple. The horse that dunk his mouth in the water to drink, and splashes the water, is a young horse that has not yet learned. And the horse who clears the water with his lips, smells the water, and then slowly sips the water to drink, this is the older horse. One who has learned the valuable, and most harsh, lessons of the desert. The other horses have learned some, however, many lessons yet remain for them.

...And so, in the old time, when the age of the horse was not known, this is how the age of the horse was determined in the desert.

Hikayat Al Maulood
The Story of the One Born

The Bedouin tribes travel from section

to section in the whole

Arabian peninsula, not strictly

one country, but the entire

Arabian world, the Middle East.

They are Nomads. And when

a tribe stops in an area, an oasis,

to rest, it is for certain reason. It may be

to gather food and water, and too,

if a mare is ready to foal.

The word Badawi, or Bedouin, is a term to describe the person that travels from section to section in the whole Arabian Peninsula. The Bedouins are the Nomads whom the desert belongs to. They have no borders. They travel from country to country. At the cities they are always welcomed. They are always respected. But the desert is their home. And when they travel, they travel like the wind. They go with their people and their possessions; their young, their old, their women, their men, their sheep, their camels, and of course, their Arabian horses.

A tribe always stopped in an area, after a long journey, where there is water, where there is shade. And they always stopped because of a reason. Maybe one of the reasons is they want to meet another tribe, or perhaps to witness the marriage of a certain daughter of a tribal leader, or maybe they wanted to trade goods from a particular area for other necessary goods. Or, one of the main reasons would be if a mare is ready to foal. Never will they travel when there is such a happening, because to the Bedouin, one of the most important things in life is the birth of a foal. So when a mare is ready to foal, the tribe will stop. And many years ago, in one of my travels to the desert, I was fortunate to witness one such happening.

At this time, the Iyaad tribe was coming from Saudi Arabia, traveling through Jordan, near to Iraq, and through the Syrian Desert, to go toward northern Syria. They were trying to reach an area between Homs and Hama, which is in Syria. It is a flat place where there is water and plenty of shade, an oasis. Tribes were always welcomed here. It is an area, a center crossing, for the Bedouins who are coming from the West and the East, and from the North and the South. The Iyaad tribe were going to stop in this area because one of their mares was soon to foal.

And the importance of this mare, and the birth of this foal, was especially great, for the leader of the

Iyaad tribe, Abou Daoud el Iyaadi, had just lost his founding stallion, his name Antar, in a battle against a band of thieves. And the great stallion, Antar, named for a famous warrior in Islamic history, along with his master, had withstood all the fighting, had withstood the many puncture wounds, until the last of the thieves were gone. And then Antar, severely weakened, dropped to his knees, and then lay down to his side. Himself wounded, Abou Daoud el Iyaadi stayed with his beloved Antar, who lay here, dying in his arms. The stallion took shallow, laboring breath until, carried by the desert wind, the spirit of the great warrior stallion returned to his creator, Allah. It was said the cry of Abou Daoud el Iyaadi could be heard for miles. So the tribe buried Antar with ceremony, and then continued on their travels, for they had one mare, a most beautiful and elegant mare, carrying the foal by Antar. And the mare was called Nour Al Oyoun, The Light of the Eyes, for her beauty shone like a bright ray of sunshine.

When the Bedouins reached the oasis, one could see Nour Al Oyoun was weary, and near ready to foal. Abou Daoud el Iyaadi led the mare to his tent, and he stayed with her. His presence seemed to have a calming affect on her. He did not touch her, but was there if she should need him. He was devoted to her in much the same way Arabian horses are devoted to their masters. This mare was certainly special. As her labor neared you could see she was not comfortable. Abou Daoud el Iyaadi spoke softly to her,

"Do not worry my love. You are safe from harm.
You have been Blessed with this new life.
Let your foal be born."

As darkness approached, and all was quiet, the dim light illuminated from the lantern in the tent, reflecting the shadow of Abou Daoud el Iyaadi, as he kneeled next to Nour Al Oyoun. Beads of sweat poured from the mare as she labored, her breath heavy. She stood, pawed the ground, and then lay down. Many times did she do this. You could see the pain in her large, soft eyes. And then, in a moment, there he was. There is born the foal, a colt, son of Antar. And Nour Al Oyoun lay there, with her foal nuzzled on her back leg, still breathing very hard, exhausted. Abou Daoud el Iyaadi removed the turban from upon his head, and carefully began to dry the foal.

After a time, Nour Al Oyoun stood to her feet, and ever so slowly, turned toward her newly born foal, reaching her long neck down to him. She breathed in deeply this strange, new scent, and then gently nudged the colt. Startled, the foal, with great effort, stood on his wobbly feet, but only for a moment, before he came crashing back to the ground. And he tried this over and over, until, at last, he was able to stand. And what a beautiful sight to see. Nour Al Oyoun then positioned herself so her foal would begin to suckle. With her gentle touch, she placed her delicate muzzle under his tail, and nudged the foal toward her udder.

The rest of the tribe, meanwhile, were waiting in anticipation to see when the mare and her foal were going to appear. After a while, with no halter and no lead, the proud mare came through the tent opening with her eyes wide open, her nostrils wide open, and making a soft murmur sound, as though she was telling her foal, "Come, there is people waiting to meet you". And then suddenly, with his four long legs, the foal came prancing out of the tent. Nour Al Oyoun and her foal went into the circle of people. The foal loped around for a time or two, almost like showing himself off. He went to his mother, took two sips of milk, and then created a little whinny, leaping happily into the air.

Abou Daoud el Iyaadi shouted to the crowd, "Behold! Look closely upon this Blessed gift from Allah.
A colt is born to us, son of Antar.
And Allah has touched this being.
Look upon his shoulder and you will see a small heart, like a dimple, where Allah has touched this foal.
This is the mark that God has given this foal."

And Abou Daoud el Iyaadi had in his hand a woven necklace made of blue color with small black beads, the watcheyes. The foal walked to Abou

Daoud el Jyaadi, stood before him, and as though he knew him for a lifetime, faithfully lowered his head. Carefully, Abou Daoud el Jyaadi slipped the necklace around the neck of the foal, and as he did this, he said,

"Hamdallah, Praise be to God. Oh, Allah.
Protect him, care for him, let no harm come to him."

It was as though for one moment, one glorious moment, that all attention were on that foal. All the hopes were on that foal. And all in the tribe that night went to their tents, very content that God blessed them with such a wonderful gift.

This is the beauty of owning an Arabian horse. For the Arab people, the Bedouins, it is very important that a horse, or a foal, be well respected by all of the tribe and beyond. Their wealth is not how much they own in gold, but their wealth is measured by their Arabian horses. And even yet today, the Jyaad tribe survives the harsh deserts of the Middle East, well respected, with their beautiful and loyal Arabian horses.

Authentic

Arabian Horse Names

SPECIAL NOTE

El or *Al*, meaning *THE*, could be used preceding most names to give
the horse more *Admiration, Dignity*, and *Power*.

For Example:
El Mahrouss (colt): The Protected One
Al Sharifah(filly): The Noble One

Ibn (Son of), and Bint (Daughter of), could precede
the name to *Honor*, or *Give A Closeness To* a founding mare or stallion.

For Example:
Ibn Al Battal: Son Of The Hero
Bint El Nil: Daughter Of The Nile

Bint Bint Sakr: Granddaughter Of The Eagle
Ibn Ibn Sawdah: Grandson Of The Black One

Some words can be used in combination for a more descriptive name.

For Example:
Koublat Al Zilal: Kiss Of The Shadow

Mares of the Shammar Bedouin tribe, 1996, photo © Joe Ferriss

Using the Dictionary

This dictionary is divided into two sections:
Arabic-English and English-Arabic.
In observing the headings at the top of each page
you will note that all of the left hand pages are
"Mouher" or names for the colt, in the masculine form.
Likewise all of the right hand pages are
"Mouhra" or names for the filly in the feminine form.
Words are listed alphabetically with each letter of
the alphabet having its own heading for easy use.

The translation column gives only a word or two
in English, however readers are encouraged to consider
the larger possibilities of these words in considering a
potential Arabic name for their newborn foal.
For instance, one might see the word: Nargileh
which means "water pipe" and wonder why
one would name their foal after a water pipe.
But the water pipe is part of an ancient tradition of social
gathering for friendship and exchange while smoking tobacco.
Even today Bedouin tribesmen, after a long, hard day can be
seen along the roadside at sunset sitting down with friends
to smoke the Nargileh, which is often filled with fruit flavored
tobacco, telling stories of the day while enjoying the peaceful
approach of dusk. Perhaps you have a filly that enjoys hanging
around you by the fence at the end of the day in similar fashion.

Furthermore, many discussions may arise concerning the
correct pronunciation of these names. Each argument may
certainly be valid as the names come from many Arabic
dialects including Syrian, Jordanian, Lebanese, and Egyptian.
With so many beautiful Arabic names for horses—their sounds
like music to one's ears—there will be many possible
connotations and combinations to ponder while enjoying the
dictionary part of this book, so do not hesitate to use your
imagination in choosing the perfect name for your horse.

Arabic-English

The Arab!

His bearing is proud,
Almost to the point of arrogance,
With an expressive head more beautiful than that
Of any other breed. It is of him that
The Koran says,

"The expression in a horse's eye is like a blessing
on a good man's house"

–THE HOLY KORAN

Mouher (Colt)

ARABIC		PRONUNCIATION	TRANSLATION
	– A –		
AAWAR	أعور	AAH-WAHR	ONE-EYED
ABDALLAH	عبدالله	AHB-DAH-LAH	GOD'S SERVANT
ABYAD	أبيض	AHB-YAHD	WHITE
ADEEB	أديب	AH-DEEB	WELL BEHAVED
ADIB	أديب	AH-DEEB	POLITE
AHDAB	أحدب	AH-DAHB	HUNCHED BACK
AHLAM	أحلام	AH-LAHM	DREAMS
AHRAM	أهرام	AH-RAHM	PYRAMID
AJDAD	أجداد	AHJ-DAD	ANCESTOR, GRANDFATHER
AJOUZ	عجوز	AH-JOOZ	OLD ONE
AKEED	أكيد	AH-KEED	FOR SURE, CERTAIN
AL AHMAR	الأحمر	AHL-AH-MAHR	THE RED ONE, THE BAY
AL ASFAR	الأصفر	AHL-AHS-FAHR	THE YELLOW
AL BATAL	البطل	AHL-BAH-TAHL	THE HERO
AL DAR	الدار	AHL-DAHR	THE COURT OF A HOUSE
AL FADEE	الفدي	AHL-FAH-DEE	THE REDEEMER
AL HADAF	الهدف	AHL-HAH-DAHF	THE GOAL
AL HADIYEH	الهدية	AHL-HAH-DEE-YEH	THE GIFT
AL JABAL	الجبل	AHL-JAH-BAL	THE MOUNTAIN
AL JASSOUS	الجاسوس	AHL-JAH-SOOS	THE SPY
AL KABEER	الكبير	AHL-KAH-BEER	THE GREAT ONE
AL KHAMSAH	الخمسة	AHL-KHAHM-SAH	THE FIVE
AL KHAMSEH	الخمسة	AHL-KAHM-SEH	THE FIVE ONES
AL MAAROUFF	المعروف	AHL-MAH-ROOF	THE WELL-KNOWN ONE

Mouhra (Filly)

ARABIC		PRONUNCIATION	TRANSLATION
	– A –		
ADEEBAH	أديبة	AH-DEE-BAH	WELL BEHAVED
ADIBEH	أديبة	AH-DEE-BEH	POLITE
AHLAM	أحلام	AH-LAHM	DREAMS
AHLIEH	أهلية	AHL-LEE-YEH	DOMESTIC
AJOUZEH	عجوزة	AH-JOOZ-EH	OLD ONE
AKEEDAH	أكيدة	AH-KEE-DAH	CERTAIN, FOR SURE
AKIDEH	أكيدة	AH-KEE-DEH	FIRM, CERTAIN
AL ARABIA	العربية	AHL-AR-RAH-BEE-YAH	THE ARAB MARE
AL BAHIEH	البهية	AHL-BAH-HEE-YEH	THE SHINING ONE
AL HADBAH	الحدباء	AHL-HAHD-BAH	THE HUNCHBACK
AL HADIYEH	الهدية	AHL-HAH-DEE-YEH	THE GIFT
AL HAMRAH	الحمرة	AHL-HAHM-RAH	THE RED ONE, THE BAY
AL JASSOUSSAH	الجاسوسة	AHL-JAH-SOO-SSAH	THE SPY
AL KABEERAH	الكبيرة	AHL-KAH-BEE-RAH	THE GREAT ONE
AL KELMAT	الكلمة	AHL-KEL-MAHT	THE WORD
AL KHAMSE	الخمسة	AHL-KAHM-SEH	THE FIVE ONES
AL MADINAH	المدينة	AHL-MAH-DEE-NAH	THE TOWN
AL MAHROUSSE	المحروسة	AHL-MAH-ROO-SSEH	THE PROTECTED ONE
AL NEFOUS	النفوس	AHL-NOU-FOOS	THE SOUL
AL RABIAH	الرابية	AHL-RAH-BEE-YAH	THE GARDEN
AL SAFIAT	الصافية	AHL-SAH-FEE-YAHT	THE PURE ONE
AL SAFNAH	الصفراء	AHL-SAHF-NAH	THE YELLOW ONE
AL SAMRAH	السمرة	AHL-SAHM-RAH	THE TANNED ONE
AL SHABHAH	الشبحة	AHL-SHAB-HAH	THE GREY ONE

Mouher (Colt)

ARABIC	PRONUNCIATION	TRANSLATION
– A –		
AL MARJ	AHL-MAHRJ	THE FIELD
AL QUASR	AHL-QUASR	THE PALACE
AL SABIL	AHL-SAH-BEEL	THE ROAD
AL SHAM	AHL-SHAM	DAMASCUS (SYRIA'S CAPITAL)
AL SHARIF	AHL-SHAH-REEF	THE NOBLE ONE
AL SHAYIB	AHL-SHAH-YEEB	THE GRAY ONE
AL WAHEED	AHL-WHAH-HEED	THE ONLY ONE (ALLAH)
AL WATTAN	AHL WHAH TAHN	THE COUNTRY
ALATOUL	AHL-LA-TOOL	FOREVER
ALI	AH-LEE	ELEVATED ONE
AL KHALI	AHL-KAH-LEE	EMPTY
ALWAN	AHL-WAHN	COLORS
AMAL	AH-MAHL	HOPE
AMAL AL OYOUN	AH-MAHL-AHL—OU-YOUN	THE APPLE OF THE EYES
AMAL HAYATI	AH-MAHL-HAH-YAH-TEE	THE WISH OF MY LIFE
AMAR	AH-MAHR	MOON
AMEEN	AH-MEEN	TRUSTWORTHY
AMIN	AH-MEEN	LOYAL, BEST FRIEND
AMIR	AH-MEER	PRINCE, KING
AMRAK	AHM-RAHK	AT YOUR ORDER OR SERVICE
ANANIYAT	AH-NAH-NEE-YAHT	EGOTISTIC
ANID	AH-NEED	STUBBORN
ANIS	AH-NEES	KIND, GOOD HEARTED, GENTLE
ANTAR	AHN-TAR	STRONG ONE, WARRIOR

Mouhra (Filly)

ARABIC		PRONUNCIATION	TRANSLATION
	– A –		
AL SHAMAH	أثامة	AHL-SHAH-MAH	THE MARK OF BEAUTY
AL SHARIFAH	أثارفة	AHL-SHAH-REEF-AH	THE NOBLE ONE
AL ZARKA	أرزقة	AHL-ZAHR-KAH	THE BLUISH-GRAY ONE
ALEEYAH	عالية	AH-LEE-YAH	SUPERIOR
ALIAH	عالية	AH-LEE-YAH	ELEVATED ONE
ALMASE	ألماس	AHL-MAH-SEH	DIAMOND
ALWAN	ألوانة	AHL-WAHN	COLORS
AMAL	أمل	AH-MAHL	HOPE
AMAL AL ARAB	أمل العرب	AH-MAHL-AHL-AH-RAHB	THE HOPE OF THE ARAB
AMAL AL OYOUN	أمل العيونه	AH-MAHL-AHL-OU-YOON	THE HOPE OF THE EYES
AMAL HAYATI	أمل حياتي	AH-MAHL-HAH-YAH-TEE	THE HOPE OF MY LIFE
AMEENAH	أمينة	AH-MEE-NAH	TRUSTWORTHY FRIEND
AMINEH	أمينة	AH-MEEN-EH	MOST TRUSTED FRIEND
AMIRAH	أميرة	AH-MEER-AH	PRINCESS
AMIRAT AL ALWAN	أميرة الألوانه	AH-MEER-AHT-AL-AHL-WAHN	PRINCESS OF THE COLORS
AMREK	أمرك	AHM-REK	AT YOUR ORDER
AMURRAH	أمورة	AH-MOUR-RAH	CUTE AS THE MOON
ANANIYAT	أنانية	AH-NAH-NEE-YAHT	EGOTISTIC
ANEESAH	أنيسة	AH-NEES-SAH	KIND, GENTLE, GOOD HEARTED
ANIDEH	عنيدة	AH-NEED-EH	STUBBORN
ANISAH	أنيسة	AH-NEES-SAH	SOCIABLE, FRIENDLY
ARMALEH	أرملة	AR-MAH-LEH	WIDOW
AROUSSAH	عروسة	AH-ROOS-SAH	BRIDE
ASILEH	عسيلة	AH-SEE-LEH	PURE

Mouher (Colt)

ARABIC		PRONUNCIATION	TRANSLATION
	– A –		
ARISS	عريس	AH-REES	BRIDEGROOM
ASHQUAR	أشقر	AHSH-KAR	CHESTNUT
ASIL	عسيل	AH-SEEL	PURE
ASLEE	أصلي	AHS-LEE	FUNDAMENTAL
ASMAR	أسمر	AHS-MAR	DARK COMPLEXION
ASSAD	أسد	AH-SSAHD	LION
ASSEER	أسير	AH-SEER	PRISONER
ASWAD	أسود	AS-WAHD	BLACK
AWALEE	أوالي	AH-WAH-LEE	ORIGINAL
AWWAL	أول	AHW-WAHL	FIRST
AZEEZ	عزيز	AH-ZEEZ	DEAR TO SOMEONE
AZIM	عظيم	AH-ZEEM	MAGNIFICENT, BOSS
AZIZ	عزيز	AH-ZEEZ	CLOSENESS TO SOMEONE
AZRAFF	أزرفه	AZ-RAHF	ELEGANT
	– B –		
BADAL	بدل	BAH-DAHL	SUBSTITUTE
BADAWI	بدوي	BAH-DAH-WEE	BEDOUIN, NOMAD
BADR	بدر	BAHDER	FULL MOON
BAHI	باهي	BAH-HEE	VIVID
BAHIJ	بهيج	BAH-HEEJ	PLEASANT
BAHLAWAN	بهلوانة	BAH-LAH-WAHN	ROPE DANCER
BAKI	باكي	BAH-KEE	TEARFUL
BAKKIR	بكير	BAHK-KEER	EARLY

Mouhra (Filly)

ARABIC		PRONUNCIATION	TRANSLATION
		– A –	
ASIRA	أسيرة	AH-SEE-RAH	PRISONER
ASLEEYAH	أصيلة	AHS-LEE-YAH	FUNDAMENTALIST
ASSEEFAH	عصيفة	AHS-SEE-FAH	STORM
AWALIYAH	أولية	AH-WAH-LEE-YAH	ORIGINAL
AWRAH	عورة	AHW-RAH	ONE-EYED
AWWALEH	أولي	AHW-WAH-LEH	FIRST
AYAR	أيار	AH-YAHR	MAY
AYLOUL	أيلول	AY-LOOL	SEPTEMBER
AZALEH	أزاله	AH-ZAH-LEH	ETERNAL
AZEEZAH	عزيزة	AH-ZEE-ZAH	DARLING, DEAR TO SOMEONE
AZEEZAT HAYATI	عزيزة حياتي	AH-ZEE-ZAHT-HAH-YAH-TEE	THE DARLING OF MY LIFE
AZIMEH	عظيمة	AH-ZEE-MEH	MAGNIFICENT, BOSS
AZIZAH	عزيزة	AH-ZEE-ZAH	CLOSENESS TO, SPECIAL BOND
AZRAH	عزراء	AHZ-RAH	VIRGIN
		– B –	
BAB EL SAMAH	باب السماء	BAWB-EL-SAH-MAH	THE DOOR OF HEAVEN
BADAWIEH	بداوية	BAH-DAH-WEE-YEH	BEDOUIN, NOMAD
BADIEH	بادية	BAH-DEE-YEH	DESERT
BAHEEJAH	بهيجة	BAH-HEE-JAH	PLEASANT
BAHIEH	بهية	BAH-HEE-YEH	SHINING, BEAUTIFUL
BAHIYAH	بهية	BAH-HEE-YAH	VIVID
BAHSEETAH	بسيطة	BAH-SEE-TAH	SIMPLE
BAIDAH SHU BAIDAH	بيضة شو بيضة	BAHY-DAH-SHOO-BAHY-DAH	WHITE, SO WHITE

Mouher (Colt)

ARABIC		PRONUNCIATION	TRANSLATION
	– B –		
BAKSHEESH	نخشيش	BAHK-SHEESH	TIP
BALADEE	بلدي	BAH-LAH-DEE	FROM THE COUNTRY
BALADI	بلدي	BAH-LAH-DEE	FROM THE COUNTRY
BALADI WE HELOU	بلدي وحلو	BAH-LAH-DEE-WEH-HEH-LOO	SIMPLE AND BEAUTIFUL
BALASH	بلاش	BAH-LAHSH	FREE
BALEED	بليد	BAH-LEED	LAZY
BALEED WE RADEE	بليد وراضي	BAH-LEED-WEH-RAH-DEE	LAZY AND CONTENT
BALGAMI	بلغامي	BAHL-GAH-MEE	MUDDY
BANDOUK	بندوقه	BAN-DOOK	BASTARD
BANI	باني	BAH-NEE	PEOPLE OF
BARAKAT	بركات	BAH-RAH-KAHT	BENEDICTION
BARD	برد	BARD	COLD
BARED AL NAHFS	بارد النفس	BAH-RED-AHL-NAHFS	THE COLD HEARTED ONE
BARIZ	باريز	BAH-REEZ	PROMINENT
BARMEEL	برميل	BAHR-MEEL	BARREL
BAROUD	بارود	BAH-ROOD	GUN POWDER
BARRANI	براني	BAH-RAH-NEE	OUTSIDER
BASEET	بسيط	BAH-SEET	SIMPLE, QUIET, LAID BACK
BASHAR	بشار	BAH-SHAHR	BEARER OF GOOD NEWS
BASHIR	بشير	BAH-SHEER	BEARER OF GOOD NEWS
BASHOOSH	باشوش	BAH-SHOOSH	ANIMATED, PLAYFUL
BASSAR	بصار	BAH-SAHR	FORTUNE TELLER
BASSBOUSS	بصبوص	BAHSS-BOOSS	PUPIL (OF THE EYE)
BATTAL	بطل	BAH-TAHL	HERO

62

Mouhra (Filly)

ARABIC		PRONUNCIATION	TRANSLATION

– B –

ARABIC	Arabic script	PRONUNCIATION	TRANSLATION
BAKIYAH	باكية	BAH-KEE-YAH	TEARFUL
BALADIEH	بلدية	BAH-LAH-DEE-YEH	FROM THE COUNTRY
BALADIEH WAH HELWEH	وحلوة	BAH-LAH-DEE-YEH-WAH-HEL-WEH	SIMPLE AND BEAUTIFUL
BALASH	بلاش	BAH-LASH	FREE
BALEEDAH	بليدة	BAH-LEE-DAH	LAZY, INACTIVE
BALGAMIYAH	بلغامية	BAHL-GAH-MEE-YAH	MUDDY
BANAFSAJI	بنفسجي	BAH-NAHF-SAH-GEE	VIOLET
BARAKAT	بركات	BAH-RAH-KAHT	BENEDICTION
BARAKEH	بركة	BAH-RAH-KEH	BLESSING
BAREDAT AL NAFS	باردة النفس	BAH-REE-DAHT-AHL-NAHFS	THE COLD HEARTED ONE
BARIZAH	بريزة	BAH-REE-ZAH	PROMINENT
BARKEH	بركة	BAR-KEH	GATHERING
BAROUDEH	بارودة	BAHR-ROO-DEH	GUN, RIFLE
BARRANIYAH	برانية	BAH-RAH-NEE-YAH	OUTSIDER
BARRIEH	برية	BAHR-REE-YEH	DESERT
BASEETAH	بسيطة	BAH-SEE-TAH	QUIET, LAID BACK
BASHARAH	بشارة	BAH-SHAH-RAH	BRINGS GOOD NEWS
BASHASHAH	بشاشة	BAH-SHAH-SHAH	CHEERFUL OR GENTLE FACE
BASHOOSHAH	بشوشة	BAH-SHOO-SHAH	ANIMATED, PLAYFUL
BASSARAH	بصارة	BAH-SAH-RAH	FORTUNE TELLER
BASSBOUSSAH	بصبوصة	BASS-BOO-SSAH	PUPIL (OF THE EYE)
BATALEH	بطلة	BAH-TAH-LEH	HEROINE
BAWAHBAH	بوابة	BAH-WAH-BAH	DOORWOMAN
BAYDAH	بيضة	BAHY-DAH	WHITE

Mouher (Colt)

ARABIC		PRONUNCIATION	TRANSLATION
– B –			
BAWAHB	بواب	BAH-WAHB	DOORMAN
BAZAR	بزار	BAH-ZAHR	MARKET
BIKR	بكر	BEEKR	FIRST BORN
BIRJ	برج	BURJ	TOWER
BITRAN	بطرانة	BIT-RAHN	EXCITED, UPSET, UNSETTTLED
BOOLBOOL	بولبول	BOOL-BOOL	CANARY
BOUKRA	بوكر	BOO-KRAH	TOMORROW
BOULAD	بولاد	BOO-LAD	METAL, LEAD
BOULBOUL	بولبول	BOOL-BOOL	NIGHTINGALE
BOUSTANI	بوستاني	BOOS-TAH-NEE	GARDENER
BUNIAT	بونية	BOO-NEE-AHT	FOUNDATION
BURJ	برج	BOORJ	TOWER
BURKAN	بركانة	BOUR-KAHN	VOLCANO
– D –			
DABBOUS	دابوس	DAHB-BOOS	PIN
DAHBOOR	دابور	DAH-BOOR	WASP
DAHHAN	دهانة	DAH-HAN	PAINTER
DAHI	داهي	DAH-HEE	SLY
DAHIYAT	داهية	DAH-HEE-YAHT	TROUBLE, CALAMITY
DAHLIL HAYATI	داليل حياتي	DAH-LEEL-HAH-YAH-TEE	GUIDE FOR MY LIFE
DAHMAR	دهمر	DAH-MAHR	EXTERMINATOR
DAHR	دهر	DAHR	TIME, AGE
DAHWALEE	دوالي	DAH-WAH-LEE	VINE

Mouhra (Filly)

ARABIC		PRONUNCIATION	TRANSLATION
BIKRAH	بكرة	BEEK-RAH	FIRST BORN
BINT AL RIYAH	بنت الرياح	BINT-AHL-REE-YAH	DAUGHTER OF THE WIND
BINT EL NIL	بنت النيل	BINT-EL-NEEL	DAUGHTER OF THE NILE
BINT EL SALAM	بنت السلام	BINT-EL-SAH-LAHM	DAUGHTER OF THE PEACE
BINT HELWAH	بنت حلوة	BINT-HEL-WAH	BEAUTIFUL GIRL, BEAUTIFUL DAUGHTER
BINT SABIYEH	بنت صبية	BINT -SAH-BEE-YEH	YOUNG GIRL, YOUNG DAUGHTER
BITRAHNEH	بطرانة	BIT-RAH-NEH	EXCITED, UPSET, UNSETTLED
BIZREH	بزرة	BIZ-REH	GRAIN, SEED
BOURHAH	برهة	BOOR-HAH	PAUSE IN TIME
BOUROUZ	بروز	BOO-ROOZ	APPEARANCE
BOUSHRAH	بشرة	BOOSH-RAH	GOOD ANNOUNCEMENT
BULBULAH	بلبولة	BOOL-BOO-LAH	CANARY
BURJ	برج	BOORJ	TOWER
BURKAN	بركانة	BOUR-KAHN	VOLCANO

– D –

ARABIC		PRONUNCIATION	TRANSLATION
DABAB	دباب	DAH-BAHB	MIST, THIN CLOUD
DABKEH	دبكة	DAHB-KEH	ORIENTAL DANCE
DABOORAH	دبورة	DAH-BOO-RAH	WASP
DAHANEH	دهانة	DAH-HAH-NEH	PAINTER
DAHIAT	داهية	DAH-HEE-YAHT	CERTAINTY, WITHOUT A DOUBT
DAHIYAH	داهية	DAH-HEE-YAH	SLY
DAHIYAT	داهيات	DAH-HEE-YAHT	CALAMITY, TROUBLE
DAHLILAT HAYATI	دليلة حياتي	DAH-LEE-LAHT-HAH-YAH-TEE	GUIDE FOR MY LIFE
DAHSHAT	دهشة	DAH-SHAHT	CONFUSION

Mouher (Colt)

ARABIC		PRONUNCIATION	TRANSLATION
	– D –		
DAHWAR	دوار	DAH-WAHRR	MOVE ABOUT, GO AROUND
DAHYEM	دايم	DAH-YEHM	CONTINUOUS, EVERLASTING
DAJIN	داجنة	DAH-JEEN	TAME
DAJJAL	دجال	DAH-JAHL	DECEIVER
DAJJAL ALA TOOL	دجال علاطول	DAH-JAHL-AH-LAH-TOOL	PERPETUAL LIAR
DAJJAN	دجانة	DAH-JAN	LIAR, UNTRUTHFUL
DALEEL	دليل	DAH-LEEL	GUIDE
DALLAL	دلال	DAH-LAHL	BROKER
DAMIS	داميس	DAH-MEES	DARK
DAMMAR	دقار	DAHM-MAHR	DESTRUCTIVE ONE
DAOUD	داود	DAH-OOD	DAVID
DARDAHSHE	دردشة	DAHR-DAH-SHEH	GOSSIP
DARDASHAH	دردشة	DAHR-DAH-SHAH	CHATTING, TALKING
DAR EL SALAM	دار السلم	DAR-EL-SAH-LAHM	THE HOUSE OF PEACE
DARWISH	درويش	DAHR-WEESH	DERVISH, SIMPLE
DASSAHYES	دسايس	DAH-SAH-YISS	INTRIGUE
DASSDASS	دسداس	DAHS-DAHS	LIKES TO TOUCH
DASSIM	داسيم	DAH-SEEM	FAT
DASSOUS	دادوس	DAH-SOOS	SPY
DASTOUR	دستور	DAHS-TOOR	RULE, REGULATION
DAWAR	دوار	DAH-WAHR	WANDERER, TRAVELER
DAWREE	دوري	DAHW-REE	MY TURN
DAYEM	دايم	DAH-YEM	IMMORTAL, FOREVER
DEEB	ديب	DEEB	WOLF

Mouhra (Filly)

ARABIC		PRONUNCIATION	TRANSLATION
	– D –		
DAHYEEMAH	دايمة	DAH-YEE-MAH	EVERLASTING
DAJINAH	داجينا	DAH-JEE-NAH	TAME
DAJJALEH	دجالة	DAH-JAH-LEH	DECEIVER
DAJJANEH	دجانة	DAH-JAN-NEH	LIAR, UNTRUTHFUL
DALAL	دلل	DAH-LAHL	TO BE SPOILED
DALEELAH	دليلة	DAH-LEE-LAH	GUIDE
DALEEYAT	دالية	DAH-LEE-YAHT	VINE
DALIAT	داليت	DAH-LEE-YAHT	GRAPEVINE
DALLALLEH	دلالة	DAH-LAH-LEH	BROKER
DAMAA	دمعة	DAHM-MAH	TEAR
DAMAZAT	دامازات	DAH-MAH-ZAHT	GENTLENESS
DAMEER	دامير	DAH-MEER	SECRET THOUGHT
DAMMARAH	دمارة	DAHM-MAH-RAH	DESTRUCTIVE ONE
DAR AL BAIDAH	دار البضة	DAHR-AHL-BAY-DAH	THE WHITE HOUSE
DARDASHA	دردشة	DAHR-DAH-SHAH	CHATTING, TALKING
DAROURAT	درورة	DAH-ROO-RAHT	NECESSITY
DARWISHAH	درويشة	DAR-WEE-SHAH	DERVISH, SIMPLE
DASSDASSAH	دلساسة	DAHS-DAH-SAH	ONE WHO LIKES TO TOUCH
DASSIMEH	داسيمة	DAH-SEE-MEH	FAT
DASSOUSSEH	داسوسة	DAH-SOOS-SEH	SPY
DAWARAH	دوارة	DAH-WAHR-AH	TRAVELER, WANDERER
DAWARAT AL BEELAD	البيلاد	DAH-WAHR-AHT-AHL-BEE-LAHD	THE TRAVELER OF THE COUNTRY
DAYEEMAH	دايمة	DAH-YEE-MAH	CONTINUOUS
DAYIMAH	دايمة	DAH-YEE-MAH	FOREVER, IMMORTAL

67

Mouher (Colt)

ARABIC		PRONUNCIATION	TRANSLATION
– D –			
DEEBAJ	ديباج	DEE-BAHJ	BROCADE
DEEN	دينه	DEEN	RELIGION
DEIFALLAH	ضيفالله	DEIYF-AL-LAH	GUEST OF GOD
DEIFI	ضيفي	DEIY-FEE	MY GUEST
DERHAM	درهم	DER-HAHM	MONEY
DIBAJ	ديباج	DEE-BAHJ	SILK BROCADE
DINAR	دينار	DEE-NAHR	GOLD COIN
DINYAWEE	دينيوية	DIN-YAH-WEE	WORDLY
DOOLAB	دولاب	DOO-LAHB	WHEEL
DOUHOUR	دهور	DOO-HOOR	TIMES, AGES
DOUKANJEE	دكاني	DOO-KAHN-JEE	SHOPKEEPER
– E –			
EBLIS	إبليس	EB-LYSS	DEVIL
EBRIZ	إبريز	EB-RIZ	PURE GOLD
EFRANJE	إفرنجي	IF-FRAN-JEE	EUROPEAN MAN
EILA AL ABAD	إلالابد	EELAH-AL-AH-BAHD	ETERNAL, FOREVER, ENDLESS
EILAT	إيلات	EE-LAHT	PORT IN ISRAEL
EJAR	إجار	EH-JAHR	LEASE, HIRE, RENT
EKTIBAR	إختبار	ICK-TEE-BAHR	EXPERIMENT
EKTILAF	إختلافه	ICK-TEE-LAHF	VARIATION
EL AAWAR	ألاعور	EL-AH-WAHR	THE ONE-EYED COLT
EL AZRAK	ألازرقه	EL-AHZ-RAHK	THE BLUISH-GREY ONE
EL MAHROUSS	ألمحروس	EL-MAH-ROOSS	THE PROTECTED ONE

Mouhra (Filly)

ARABIC		PRONUNCIATION	TRANSLATION
– D –			
DAYIMAH WAYAYAH	ديمةواياية	DAH-YEE-MAH-WAH-YAH-YAH	TO STAY WITH ME FOREVER
DEEBAH	ديبة	DEE-BAH	WOLF
DIBAJEH	ديباجة	DEE-BAH-JEH	SILK BROCADE
DIBBANI	دبانة	DEEB-BAH-NEE	COLORATION FLEA BITTEN GREY
DIEFEE	ضيفي	DEIY-FEE	MY GUEST
DIMASHK	دمشق	DEE-MASHK	DAMASCUS
DINYAWIYAH	دنياوية	DIN-YAH-WEE-YAH	WORLDLY
DIRAYAT	دراية	DEER-AH-YAHT	KNOWLEDGE
DOUHMAT	دهمة	DOOH-MAHT	BLACKNESS
DOUNIAH	دنية	DOO-NEE-AH	PRESENT WORLD
DUHUUR	دهور	DOO-HOOR	DECADE, TIME PASSED
DUNYAH	دنية	DOON-YAH	WORLD
– E –			
EBRA	إبرة	EB-RAH	NEEDLE
EFRANJIYEH	إفرنجية	IF-FRAN-JEE-YEH	EUROPEAN WOMAN
EL AJOUZ	العجوز	EL-AH-JOOZ	THE OLD ONE
EL AWRAH	العورة	EL-OUW-RAH	THE ONE EYED MARE OR FILLY
ELA EIN	إلى اينه	EELAH-EIN	WHERE?
ELFAT	إلفة	EL-FAHT	FRIENDSHIP
ELHAM	إلهام	EL-HAM	INSPIRATION
EMARAT	إمارات	EE-MAH-RAHT	COUNTRIES UNITED
EMEERA	أميرة	EH-MEE-RAH	PRINCESS
EMIRA	اميرة	EH-MEE-RAH	PRINCESS
ESMAKEE	إسماكي	ISS-MAH-KEE	YOUR NAME IS?

Mouher (Colt)

ARABIC		PRONUNCIATION	TRANSLATION
	– E –		
EL MAREES	ألمارس	EL-MAHR-REES	THE SOUTH WIND
EL NIL	ألنيل	EL-NEEL	THE NILE
EL SARAYA	ألسراية	EL-SAH-RAH-YAH	THE COURTHOUSE
EMAN	إمانه	EE-MAHN	CREED, BELIEF
EMEER	أمير	EH-MEER	PRINCE
EMIR	امير	EH-MEER	PRINCE
ESMAK	إسمك	ISS-MAC	YOUR NAME IS?
ETTIZAN	إتزانه	IT-TEEZ-AHN	EQUILIBRIUM
EWAN	إوانه	EE-WAHN	PORCH, HALL
EYAB	إياب	EE-YAHB	TO RETURN
EYAS	إيس	EE-YAHS	DESPAIR
	– F –		
FADDAN	فدانه	FAHD-DAHN	OXEN YOKE, A MEASURE
FADEE	فادي	FAH-DEE	REDEEMER
FADEL	فاضل	FAH-DELL	PERFECTION, WITHOUT FAULT
FADL	فضل	FAHDL	EXCESS FAVOR, EXCELLENCE
FADOOLEE	فادولة	FAH-DOO-LEE	GRATEFUL
FAHD	فهد	FAHD	PANTHER, LYNX
FAHEEM	فاهيم	FAH-HEEM	ALERT, SMART
FAHESH	فاحش	FAH-HESH	BULLY, EXCESSIVE
FAHIM	فاهيم	FAH-HEEM	INGENIOUS
FAHKOUR	فاخور	FAH-KOOR	PROUD
FAHL	فحل	FAH-HELL	STALLION

Mouhra (Filly)

ARABIC		PRONUNCIATION	TRANSLATION
		– F –	
FADILAT	نضيلة	FAH-DEE-LAHT	VIRTUE, EXCELLENCE
FADOOLIYAH	فاضولية	FAH-DOO-LEE-YAH	GRATEFUL
FAHDEELAH	نضيلة	FAH-DEE-LAH	PERFECTION, WITHOUT FAULT
FAHEEMEH	فاهيمة	FAH-HEE-MEH	SMART, ALERT
FAHIMAH	فاهيمة	FAH-HEE-MAH	INGENIOUS
FAHIMEH	فاهيمة	FAH-HEE-MEH	VERY INTELLIGENT, SMART
FAJEERAH	فاجرة	FAH-JEER-AH	WICKED ONE
FAKOURAH	فاخورة	FAH-KOO-RAH	PROUD
FALLAHAH	فلاحة	FAH-LAH-HAH	FARMER, COUNTRY WOMAN
FARAH	مرح	FAH-RAH	GENERAL HAPPINESS
FARASE	خراسة	FAHR-AHS-EH	MARE
FARASHAH	فراشة	FAH-RAH-SHAH	BUTTERFLY (FLOATY AND LIGHT)
FARASHEH	فراشة	FAH-RAH-SHEH	BUTTERFLY (FLOATY AND LIGHT)
FARDANIYAH	فردانية	FAHR-DAH-NEE-YAH	SINGULAR
FAREEDAH	فاريدة	FAH-REE-DAH	PRECIOUS GEM
FARESSAH	فارسة	FAHR-ESS-AH	PREY
FARHANEH	فرحانة	FAHR-HAH-NEH	HAPPY ONE, LIVELY
FARHANEH ALA TOOL	فرحانة علطول	FAHR-HAH-NEH-AH-LAH-TOOL	HAPPINESS ALWAYS
FARIDAH	فريدة	FAH-REE-DAH	EXCEPTIONAL
FARJIYAH	فرجية	FAHR-JEE-YAH	OVER GARMENT
FARMAT	فرمة	FAHR-MAHT	SMALL PIECE
FARWAT	فروة	FAHR-WAHT	FUR CLOAK
FASEEHAH	فصيحة	FAH-SEE-HAH	FLUENT IN LANGUAGE
FASHARAH	فنشارة	FAH-SHAH-RAH	SWAGGERER (CONCEITED STRUT)

Mouher (Colt)

ARABIC		PRONUNCIATION	TRANSLATION
		– F –	
FAHTER	خاتر	FAH-TEHR	LUKEWARM
FAJIR	خاجر	FAH-JEER	WICKED ONE
FAJR	فجر	FAJR	DAWN, DAYBREAK
FALAFEL	فلافل	FAH-LAH-FEL	FOOD
FALAKEE	خلاكي	FAH-LAH-KEE	ASTRONOMER, FUTURE TELLER
FALLAH	فلاح	FAH-LAH	FARMER, COUNTRYMAN
FANOUS	خانوس	FAH-NOOS	LANTERN, LAMP
FARAH	فرح	FAH-RAH	HAPPINESS
FARAJ	فرج	FAH-RAHJ	RELIEF
FARAS	فرس	FAH-RAHS	HORSE
FARASHEH	فراشة	FAH-RAH-SHEH	BUTTERFLY (LIGHT, FLOATY)
FARDANI	فرداني	FAHR-DAH-NEE	SINGULAR
FAREED	فريد	FAH-REED	ONE OF A KIND, UNIQUE
FAREES	خارس	FAH-REES	HORSEMAN
FARHAN	فرحانة	FAHR-HAHN	HAPPY, LIVELY, JUBILANT
FARID	فريد	FAH-REED	EXCEPTIONAL
FASEEH	خاصح	FAH-SEAH	FLUENT IN LANGUAGE
FASHAL	خاشل	FAH-SHALL	FAILURE
FASHAR	خاتر	FAH-SHAR	SWAGGERER (CONCEITED STRUT)
FASSED	خاسد	FAH-SSED	SPOILED, BAD
FASSHEET	خاصيط	FAH-SHEET	CONCEITED
FATEH	خاتح	FAH-TEH	CONQUEROR
FATTAL	فتال	FAHT-TAHL	ROPE MAKER, TWISTER
FAWRAN	فورانه	FAHW-RAN	AT ONCE

Mouhra (Filly)

ARABIC		PRONUNCIATION	TRANSLATION
	– F –		
FASHEETAH	ضشيطة	FAH-SHEE-TAH	CONCEITED
FASSEEDAH	فاسيدة	FAH-SEE-DAH	IMMORAL
FATTEERAH	فاطيرة	FAH-TEE-RAH	LUKEWARM
FAURAN	فورانه	FAW-RAN	AT ONCE
FAWARAH	فوارة	FAH-WAH-RAH	FOUNTAIN
FAWDA	فودة	FAHW-DAH	ANARCHY
FAYEEDAH	فايدة	FAH-YEE-DAH	USEFUL
FAYLASSOOFAH	فيلسوفة	FAY-LAH-SOU-FAH	PHILOSOPHER
FAYROUZ	فيروز	FAY-ROOZ	TURQUOISE
FAZAANEH	فزعانة	FAHZ-AAH-NEH	SCARED
FERDOUS	فردوس	FEHR-DOWS	PARADISE
FERHANEH	فرحانة	FEHR-HAHN-EH	REJOICING
FIDDAT	فيدات	FEED-DAHT	SILVER
FINJAN	فنجانه	FIN-JAHN	SMALL CUP, TEA CUP
FITNAT	فتنة	FIT-NAHT	UNDERSTANDING
FOURJAH	فورجة	FOOR-JAH	OPENING SHOW
FULFUL	فلفل	FULL-FULL	PEPPER (TREE OR FRUIT)
	– G –		
GAMILAH	جميلة	GAH-MEEL-AH	PRETTY, BEAUTIFUL
GHANOUJEH	جانوجة	GHAH-NOO-JEH	CUTE AND SASSY
GHARIBEH	جاريبة	GHA-REE-BEH	STRANGER
GHAZALEH	غزالة	GHA-ZAH-LEH	DEER, ANTELOPE
GHOUNIAT	غنية	GHOO-NEE-YAHT	MELODY

Mouher (Colt)

ARABIC		PRONUNCIATION	TRANSLATION
– F –			
FAYED	مايد	FAH-YED	USEFUL
FAYLASSOOF	فيلاسوف	FAY-LAH-SSOOF	PHILOSOPHER
FAZAAN	فزعانه	FAHZ-AHN	SCARED, FRIGHTENED
FENJAHN	فنجانه	FEN-JAHN	CUP
FERAR	فرار	FEE-RAHR	FLIGHT, ESCAPE
FERHAN	فرحانه	FEHR-HAHN	REJOICING
FINJAN KABEER	فنجانه كبير	FEEN-JAHN-KAH-BEER	LARGE CUP
FIRDOUSS	فردوس	FIR-DOUSS	PARADISE
FOONDOC	فندقه	FOON-DOC	HOTEL
FOUAD	فؤاد	FOO-ADD	HEART
FOULAZ	فولاز	FOO-LAHZ	STEEL
FOURSAN	فورسانه	FOOR-SSAN	HORSEMEN
FOURSAN AL SAHRA	الصحرة	FOOR-SSAN-AHL-SAH-RAH	THE DESERT HORSEMEN
FOUSTOK	فستقه	FOOS-TOC	PEANUTS
– G –			
GAMAL	جمال	GAH-MAHL	BEAUTY
GAMIL	جميل	GAH-MEEL	PRETTY, BEAUTIFUL
GAMIL AL OYOUN	العيونه	GAH-MEEL-AHL-OU-YOON	THE PRETTY EYED ONE
GHAFER	غفير	GAH-FER	FORGIVING
GHARB	غرب	GHA-ERB	WEST
GHARIB	غريب	GAH-REEB	STRANGER
GHAZAL	غزال	GHA-ZAHL	DEER, ANTELOPE
GHOUL	غول	GOOL	GIANT

Mouhra (Filly)

ARABIC		PRONUNCIATION	TRANSLATION

– H –

ARABIC		PRONUNCIATION	TRANSLATION
HABAYEB	حبايب	HAH-BAH-YEB	LOVED ONE
HABIBI	حبيبي	HAH-BEE-BEE	MY LOVE
HABIBTEE	حبيبتي	HAH-BEEB-TEE	DEAR, MY BELOVED
HADAYAH	هدية	HAH-DAH-YAH	GIFTS
HADBAH	حدبة	HAHD-BAH	HUNCHED BACK
HADIYAH	هادية	HAH-DEE-YAH	GIFT
HADIYAT AL NOUFOUS	النفوس	HAH-DEE-YAHT-AHL-NOO-FOOS	GIFT OF THE SPIRIT
HADIYAT AL OYOUN	العيون	HAH-DEE-YAHT-AHL-OU-YOON	GIFT OF THE EYES
HAIHAT	حيهات	HAI-HAHT	MANY HELLOS (USED IN ARABIC SONGS)
HAIRANEH	حيرانة	HAI-RAH-NEH	CURIOUS, INQUISITIVE
HAJMEH	هجمة	HAHJ-MEH	ATTACK, RUSH
HAKEMEH	حكمة	HAH-KEH-MEH	JUDGE
HAKIMAH	حكيمة	HAH-KEE-MAH	COMMANDER
HAKIMEH	حكيمة	HAH-KEE-MEH	WISE
HALA YA HALA	هلا يا هلا	HAH-LAH-YAH-HAH-LAH	WELCOME, OH WELCOME
HALAWA	حلاوة	HAH-LAH-WAH	SWEETNESS
HALIMAH	حليمة	HAH-LEE-MAH	MILD
HAMAMEE	حمامي	HAH-MAH-MEE	DOVE
HAMRAH	حمرة	HAM-RAH	BAY (COLOR)
HAMSAT	همسة	HAHM-SAHT	WHISPER
HANOONEH	حنونة	HAH-NOO-NEH	AFFECTIONATE, TENDER PASSION
HANOUNEH	حنونة	HAH-NOO-NEH	SOFT HEARTED
HARAM	حرام	HAH-RAHM	FORBIDDEN
HARAMIYEH	حرامية	HAH-RAH-MEE-YEH	THIEF

Mouher (Colt)

ARABIC		PRONUNCIATION	TRANSLATION
	– H –		
HABIB	حبيب	HAH-BEEB	LOVER, BELOVED
HADAF	حدف	HAH-DAHF	TARGET, AIM, GOAL
HADDAD	حداد	HAH-DAD	BLACKSMITH
HADDID	حديد	HAH-DEED	IRON
HADEE	حادى	HAH-DEE	QUIET
HADEER	حدير	HAH-DEER	ROCKING (OF WAVES, ETC)
HADIYA	حدية	HAH-DEE-YAH	GIFT
HADIYAT	حدية	HAH-DEE-YAHT	GIFTS
HAFEED	حفيد	HAH-FEED	GRANDSON OF
HAIKAL	هيكل	HAI-KAHL	TEMPLE
HAIRAN	حيرانة	HAI-RAHN	CURIOUS, INQUISITIVE
HAJAR	حجار	HAH-JAR	STONE
HAJJ	الحاج	HAJJ	PILGRIMAGE TO MECCA
HAKEEM	حكيم	HAH-KEEM	WISE
HAKEM	حاكم	HAH-KEM	GOVERNOR, COMMANDER
HALA YA HALA	حلا يا حلا	HAH-LAH-YAH-HAH-LAH	WELCOME, OH WELCOME
HALEEM	حليم	HAH-LEEM	MILD
HAMAM	حمام	HAH-MAHM	DOVE
HAMDALLAH	حمد الله	HAM-DAH-LAH	PRAISE BE TO GOD
HAMEE	حامى	HAH-MEE	HOT TO THE TOUCH
HAMI	حامى	HAH-MEE	PROTECTOR, GUARDIAN
HAMSAT	همسة	HAHM-SAHT	WHISPER
HANASH	حنش	HAH-NASH	SNAKE
HANOON	حنونة	HAH-NOON	AFFECTIONATE, TENDER PASSION

Mouhra (Filly)

ARABIC		PRONUNCIATION	TRANSLATION
		– H –	
HAREEM	مريم	HAH-REEM	WOMAN OF A HOUSEHOLD
HARISSAH	مريضة	HAH-REE-SSAH	PROTECTOR
HARISSEH AL HAYAT	الحياة	HAH-REE-SSEH-AL-HAH-YAHT	GUARD OF THE LIFE
HASADDEH	حسادة	HAH-SAD-DEH	JEALOUSY, ENVY
HASSANIEH	حسنية	HAHS-SAH-NEE-EH	BEAUTY
HASSENAT	هلنة	HAH-SSEH-NAHT	GOOD SEED
HATTABEH	حطابة	HAH-TAH-BEH	WOOD CUTTER
HAWAH	حوا	HAH-WAH	LOVE
HAWEEYAH	هاوية	HAH-WEE-YAH	AMATEUR
HAWIYAH	هاوية	HAH-WEE-YAH	IN LOVE
HAYEJAH	هايجة	HAH-YEH-JAH	RAGING
HAYJANNEH	هيجانة	HAY-JAH-NEH	EXCITED, EXUBERANT
HAZEEMAH	هزيمة	HAH-ZEE-MAH	ESCAPEE
HAZINEH	هزينة	HAH-ZEE-NEH	TO BE GRIEVED
HAZIRAH	حازيرة	HAH-ZEE-RAH	ENCLOSURE
HAZZALEH	حزّالة	HAH-ZAH-LEH	HUMOROUS
HAZZARAH	هزّارة	HAH-ZAH-RAH	JOKER
HAZZOURAH	حزورة	HAH-ZOO-RAH	QUIZ, TEST
HEHYAM	حيام	HEH-YAHM	PASSIONATE LOVE
HELWAH	حلوة	HEL-WAH	BEAUTIFUL, VERY ATTRACTIVE
HELWETT	حلوة	HEL-WETT	PRETTY ONE
HIJRAT	هجيرة	HEEJ-RAHT	SEPARATION, FLIGHT
HIKAYAT	حكاية	HEE-KAH-YAHT	STORY, TALE
HILAL	حلال	HEE-LAHL	MOON

Mouher (Colt)

ARABIC		PRONUNCIATION	TRANSLATION
		– H –	
HARAM	حرام	HAH-RAHM	FORBIDDEN
HARAMI	حرامي	HAH-RAH-MEE	BURGLAR, THIEF
HARESS	حارس	HAH-RESS	PROTECTOR
HARESS AL DAR	حارس الدار	HAH-RESS-AHL-DAHR	PROTECTOR OF THE HOUSE
HARIK	حريقه	HAH-REEK	FIRE
HARIS	حاريس	HAH-REES	VIGILANT, WATCHFUL
HARRIS	حاريس	HAH-REES	WORKMAN, GUARD
HASSAD	حسد	HAH-SAD	JEALOUSY, ENVY
HATTAB	حطاب	HAHT-TAB	WOODCUTTER
HAWEE	هاوي	HAH-WEE	AMATEUR
HAWI	هاوي	HAH-WEE	IN LOVE
HAYAHJAN	هيجانه	HAH-YAH-JAN	PASSION
HAYEJ	هايج	HAH-YEHJ	RAGING
HAYEM	هايم	HAH-YEM	LOVE STRICKEN
HAYJAN	هيجانه	HAY-JAHN	EXCITED, EXUBERANT
HAZAL	هزال	HAH-ZAHL	HUMOR
HAZEEM	هازيم	HAH-ZEEM	ESCAPEE
HAZEM	حازم	HAH-ZEM	PRUDENT, RESOLUTE
HAZZAL	هزال	HAH-ZZAHL	HUMOROUS
HAZZAR	هزار	HAH-ZAHR	JOKER
HELOU	حلو	HEH-LOO	PRETTY ONE
HIJAB	حجاب	HEE-JAHB	VEIL, PARTITION
HILAL	هلال	HEE-LAHL	NEW MOON, CRESCENT
HIYAHJ	هياج	HEE-YAHJ	EXCITEMENT

Mouhra (Filly)

ARABIC		PRONUNCIATION	TRANSLATION
– H –			
HIMAYAT	حمايات	HEE-MAH-YAHT	PROTECTION
HISHMAT	حشمة	HISH-MAHT	REVERENCE, MODESTY
HIYAHJ	هياج	HEE-YAHJ	EXCITEMENT
HIYAM	هيام	HEE-YAHM	LOVE, AFFECTION
HUJJAT	حجة	HUHJ-JAHT	EXCUSE, PRETEXT
– I –			
IHTEMAM	إهتمام	IH-TEE-MAM	EARNEST
IHTERAM	إهترام	IH-TEE-RAM	RESPECT, HIGH ESTEEM
IJTEHAD	إجتهاد	IJ-TEE-HAD	DILIGENCE
IKTERAB	إقتراب	IK-TEE-RAB	APPROACH, MOVE TOWARD
ILHAM	إلهام	EEL-HAM	DIRECTION FOR ALLAH
INHEEZAM	إنهزام	IN-HEE-ZAHM	DEFEAT
INKISAF	إنكساف	IN-KEE-SAHF	ECLIPSE
INSANIAT	إنسانية	IN-SAH-NEE-YAHT	HUMANITY, POLITENESS
INTE FEIN	إنتي فين	IN-TEE-FEIN	WHERE ARE YOU?
INTIZAR	إنتظار	IN-TEE-ZAR	WAITING, EXPECTATION
IRDEH	إردة	IRR-DEH	OVERLY ACTIVE, ENERGETIC
IRTIBAT	إرتباط	IR-TEE-BAHT	ASSOCIATION
ISHARAT	إشارات	E-SHAH-RAHT	SIGN
ISHTIAAL	إشتعال	ISH-TEE-AAL	IGNITION
ISPHANJE	إسفنجي	ISS-FAN-JEH	SPONGE
ISTIKBAR	إستكبار	ISS-TIK-BAR	CONCEITED, SELF ASSURED
ITTIHAD	إتحاد	IT-TEE-HAD	UNITED UNION

Mouher (Colt)

ARABIC		PRONUNCIATION	TRANSLATION

– H –

HIYAM	صيام	HEE-YAHM	LOVE, AFFECTION
HOUB	حب	HOOB	LOVE
HOUB YA HABIBI	حب ياحبيبي	HOOB-YAH-HAH-BEE-BEE	LOVE MY DARLING
HOUJOUM	هجوم	HOO-JOOM	ATTACK
HOURRIAT	حورية	HOO-REE-YAHT	FREEDOM
HUSSAM	حسام	HUH-SSAM	SHARP SWORD

– I –

IBN AL NIL	إبن النيل	IBN-AHL-NEEL	SON OF THE NILE
IBN AL RIYAH	إبنه الرياح	IBN-AHL-REE-YAH	SON OF THE WIND
IBN AL SALAM	إبنه السلام	IBN-AHL-SAH-LAHM	SON OF THE PEACE
IBN JAMEEL	إبنه جميل	IBN-JAH-MEEL	BEAUTIFUL BOY, BEAUTIFUL SON
IBN SHAABEE	إبنه شعبي	IBN-SHAA-BEE	POPULAR SON
IHTEMAM	إهتمام	IH-TEE-MAM	EARNEST
IHTERAM	إحترام	IH-TEE-RAM	RESPECT, HIGH ESTEEM
IJTEHAD	إجتهاد	IJ-TEE-HAD	DILIGENCE
IKHWAN	إخوانه	IKH-WAHN	BRETHREN
IKTIRAB	إقتراب	IK-TEE-RAB	APPROACH
ILHAM	إلهام	EEL-HAM	DIRECTION FOR ALLAH
IMAM	إمام	EE-MAM	LEADER, HOLY MAN
INFIJAR	إنفجار	IN-FEE-JAHR	EXPLOSION
INHEEZAM	إنهزام	IN-HEE-ZAM	DEFEAT
INKISAF	إنكسافه	IN-KEE-SAHF	ECLIPSE
INSANEE	إناني	IN-SAH-NEE	HUMAN

Mouhra (Filly)

ARABIC		PRONUNCIATION	TRANSLATION
	– J –		
JABBARAH	جبارة	JAH-BAH-RAH	STRONG, PROUD
JABHA	جبهة	JAHB-HAH	FOREHEAD
JADBAH	جدبة	JAHD-BAH	STERILE, BARE
JADEEDAH	جديدة	JAH-DEE-DAH	RECENT, NEW
JADEEDAH BIL HOUB	بالحب	JAH-DEE-DAH-BIL-HOOB	NEW IN LOVE
JADEEDEH	جديدة	JAH-DEE-DEH	NEW ONE
JADWAH	جدوة	JAHD-WAH	GIFT, BENEFIT
JAHANAMIYAH	جهنمية	JAH-HAH-NAH-MEE-YAH	FROM HELL
JAHEELAH	جاهلة	JAH-HEE-LAH	YOUNG AT HEART, TEENAGER
JAHILAH	جاهلة	JAH-HEE-LAH	UNKNOWING, NOT KNOWING BETTER
JAHMHOURIEH	جمهورية	JAHM-HOO-RIEH	CROWD, REPUBLIC
JAHMIDAH	جامدة	JAH-MEE-DAH	STIFF, FIRM
JAHRIAT	جارية	JAH-REE-YAHT	DAMSEL, YOUNG GIRL
JAHSEEMAH	جسيمة	JAH-SEE-MAH	BULKY, OVERSIZED
JAHSEERAH WAH ANIDAH	وعنيدة	JAH-SEE-RAH-WAH-AH-NEE-DAH	BOLD AND STUBBORN
JAHSSIMAH	جسيمة	JAH-SEE-MAH	OVERSIZED, BULKY
JAHZAHBAT	جزاءة	JAH-ZAH-BAHT	CHARM, SPELL, BEWITCH
JALALAT	جلالت	JAH-LAH-LAHT	SPLENDOR, MAJESTY
JALEELAH	جليلة	JAH-LEE-LAH	GREAT, MAGNIFICENT
JALLADEH	جلادة	JAH-LAH-DEH	EXECUTIONER
JALSAT	جلست	JAHL-SAHT	SESSION, GATHERING
JAMEELAH	جميلة	JAH-MEE-LAH	BEAUTIFUL, GRACEFUL
JAMHOURIAT	جمهورية	JAM-HOO-REE-YAHT	REPUBLIC
JAMIDAT	جامدة	JAH-MEE-DAHT	SOLID

Mouher (Colt)

ARABIC		PRONUNCIATION	TRANSLATION
		– I –	
INTIKAM	إنتقام	IN-TEE-KAHM	VENGEANCE
INTIZAR	إنتظار	IN-TEE-ZAR	WAITING, EXPECTATION
ISHARAT	اشارة	E-SHAH-RAHT	SIGN
ISHTIHAR	إشتهار	ISH-TEE-HAR	CELEBRITY
ISPHANJ	اسفنج	ISS-FANJ	SPONGE
ISTIKBAR	إستكبار	ISS-TIK-BAR	CONCEITED, SELF ASSURED
		– J –	
JABAL	جبل	JAH-BAL	MOUNTAIN
JABBAR	جبار	JAH-BAHR	STRONG, PROUD
JADEED	جديد	JAH-DEED	NEW ONE
JAHANAMEE	جهنمي	JAH-HAH-NAH-MEE	FROM HELL
JAHEL	جاهل	JAH-HEL	UNKNOWING, NOT KNOWING BETTER
JAHMED	جامد	JAH-MED	STIFF, FIRM
JAHMHOUR	جمهور	JAHM-HOOR	CROWD
JAHWHAR	جوهر	JAHW-HAR	GEM, PRECIOUS STONE
JAHZAHBAT	جزابة	JAH-ZAH-BAHT	CHARM, SPELL, BEWITCH
JALAL	جلال	JAH-LAHL	SPLENDOR, MAJESTY
JALALAT	جلالات	JAH-LAH-LAHT	YOUR MAJESTY
JALEEL	جليل	JAH-LEEL	GREAT
JALIL	جليل	JAH-LEEL	GRAND, MIGHTY
JALLAD	جلاده	JAH-LLAHD	EXECUTIONER
JAMAL	جمال	JAH-MAHL	CAMEL
JAMEEL YAH JAMEEL	يا جميل	JAH-MEEL-YAH-JAH-MEEL	BEAUTIFUL, OH BEAUTIFUL

Mouhra (Filly)

ARABIC		PRONUNCIATION	TRANSLATION
		– J –	
JAMRAT	حمرة	JAHM-RAHT	LIVE COAL
JARIYAT	جارية	JAH-REE-YAHT	SLAVE GIRL
JASOORAH	جادورة	JAH-SOO-RAH	BOLD, COURAGEOUS
JASSARA	جسارة	JAH-SAH-RAH	COURAGE
JASSIRAH	جاسية	JAH-SEE-RAH	BOLD, FORTHRIGHT
JASSIRAH WAH HELWAH	وحلوة	JAH-SEE-RAH-WAH-HEL-WAH	BOLD AND BEAUTIFUL
JAWADEH	جوادة	JAH-WAH-DEH	HORSERACER
JAWAHER	جواهر	JAH-WAH-HEHR	PRECIOUS STONE
JAWAIZ	جوائز	JAH-WAH-EZ	PRIZE, PRESENT
JAWDAT	جودات	JAHW-DAHT	GOODNESS, EXCELLENCE
JAWHARAH	جوهرة	JAHW-HAH-RAH	GEM
JAWHARAT	جوهرات	JAHW-HAH-RAHT	JEWEL, PEARL
JAYEDAH	جيدة	JAH-YEH-DAH	EXCELLENT
JAZEEBAH	جازبة	JAH-ZEE-BAH	ATTRACTIVE
JAZEELAH	جازلة	JAH-ZEE-LAH	AFFLUENT
JAZIRAH	جزيرة	JAH-ZEE-RAH	ISLAND
JEENAH	جناح	JEE-NAH	WING
JEENAH AL HAWAH	الهوا	JEE-NAH-AHL-HAW-WAH	THE WING OF LOVE
JENAYAT	جنية	JEH-NAH-YAHT	TO COMMIT A CRIME
JENOUBEE	جنوبي	JEH-NOO-BEE	SOUTHERNER
JIBBAH	جبا ه	JIB-BAH	FOREHEAD
JIHAD	جهاد	JEE-HAD	HOLY CAMPAIGN, RESISTANCE
JUNDIYAH	جندية	JUN-DEE-YAH	FEMALE MILITARY MEMBER
JUNDIYEH	جندية	JUN-DEE-YEH	FEMALE SOLDIER

Mouher (Colt)

ARABIC		PRONUNCIATION	TRANSLATION
		– J –	
JAMIL	جميل	JAH-MEEL	BEAUTIFUL
JAMR	جمر	JAHMR	ASHES, COAL
JARRAH	جراح	JAH-RAH	SURGEON
JASEEM AL SADR	جسيم الصدر	JAH-SEEM-AHL-SADR	THE BULKY CHESTED ONE
JASIM	جسيم	JAH-SEEM	BULKY
JASSARAT	جسارات	JAH-SAH-RAHT	BOLDNESS, COURAGE
JASSEHR	جسيل	JAH-SEHR	BOLD, FORTHRIGHT
JASSUR	جاسور	JAH-SOOR	COURAGEOUS
JAWAD	جواد	JAH-WAHD	HORSERACER
JAWALAN	جوالنه	JAH-WAH-LAHN	ACT OF TRAVELING ABOUT
JAYED	جايد	JAH-YED	EXCELLENT
JAZEB	جازب	JAH-ZEHB	ATTRACTIVE
JAZEEL	جازيل	JAH-ZEEL	AFFLUENT
JAZZAR	جزار	JAH-ZAHR	BUTCHER
JEEDAR	جيدار	JEE-DAHR	WALL, ENCLOSURE
JEENAH	جناح	JEE-NAH	WING
JEENAH AL HAWAH	جناح الهوى	JEE-NAH-AHL-HAH-WAH	THE WING OF LOVE
JEHAD	جهاد	JEE-HAD	COMBAT, STRUGGLE
JIHAD	جهاد	JEE-HAD	HOLY CAMPAIGN, RESISTANCE
JISR	جسر	JISER	BRIDGE
JISR AL HAWAH	جسر الهوى	JISER-AL-HAH-WAH	THE BRIDGE OF LOVE
JULJUL	جلجل	JOOL-JOOL	SMALL BELL
JUMAA	جمعة	JUHM-AAH	WEEK (7 DAYS)
JUNDEE	جندي	JUN-DEE	SOLDIER

Mouhra (Filly)

ARABIC		PRONUNCIATION	TRANSLATION
	– K –		
KABEERAH	كبيرة	KAH-BEE-RAH	GRAND
KABIREH	كبيرة	KAH-BEE-REH	GREAT SIZE, LARGE, GIANT
KADIMAH	قديمة	KAH-DEE-MAH	ANCIENT
KAFALEH	كفالة	KAH-FAH-LEH	SECURITY, BAIL
KAHFIRAH	كافرة	KAH-FEE-RAH	NON-BELIEVER
KAHILEH	أصيلة	KAH-HEE-LEH	PURE BRED, BEST BREED
KAHLIDAH	خالدة	KAH-LEE-DAH	FOREVER
KAHMAL	كمال	KAH-MAHL	INTEGRITY
KAHMILAH	كاملة	KAH-MEE-LAH	COMPLETE
KAHRAMAN	كهرمانة	KAH-RAH-MAHN	AMBER
KAHTEEBAH	كاتبة	KAH-TEE-BAH	WRITER
KAHZABEH	كذابة	KAH-ZAH-BEH	DISHONEST, LIAR
KAIMAT	خيمة	KAY-MAHT	TENT
KAMAL	كمال	KAH-MAL	HIGH DEGREE OF EXCELLENCE, PERFECTION
KAMAR	قمر	KAH-MAHR	MOON
KAMELAT AL AWSAF	كاملة الأوصاف	KAH-MEE-LAHT-AHL-AHW-SAHF	THE PERFECT DESCRIPTION
KAMIYAT	كمية	KAH-MEE-YAHT	QUANTITY
KAN YAMA KAN	كان يا ما كان	KAHN-YAH-MAH-KAHN	ONCE UPON THE TIME
KARAHMAH	كرامة	KAH-RAH-MAH	GRACIOUSNESS
KARAZEH	كرزة	KAH-RAH-ZEH	CHERRY, BEAD
KARBOUJEH	كربوجة	KAHR-BOO-JEH	CUTE, ATTRACTIVE
KAREEMAH	كريمة	KAH-REE-MAH	GIVER, KIND
KARIMAH	كريمة	KAH-REE-MAH	NOBLE, LIBERAL
KARIMEH	كريمة	KAH-REE-MEH	PRECIOUS OBJECT

Mouher (Colt)

ARABIC		PRONUNCIATION	TRANSLATION
		– K –	
KABEER	كبير	KAH-BEER	GRAND, GREAT
KABIR	كبير	KAH-BEER	LARGE, GIANT
KADEEM	قديم	KAH-DEEM	ANCIENT
KADI	قاضي	KAH-DEE	JUDGE
KAFER	كافر	KAH-FER	NON-BELIEVER
KAFIL	كفيل	KAH-FEEL	ONE WHO STANDS BAIL
KAFOUR	كافور	KAH-FOOR	CAMPHOR
KAHAR	قهار	KAH-HAHR	CONQUEROR
KAHAR AL ABTAL	الابطال	KAH-HAHR-AHL-AB-TAHL	BRAVEST OF THE BRAVE
KAHIL	كحيل	KAH-HEEL	HORSE OF BEST BREED
KAHMAL	كمال	KAH-MAHL	INTEGRITY
KAHTEB	كاتب	KAH-TEB	WRITER
KAMAL	كمال	KAH-MAHL	HIGH DEGREE OF EXCELLENCE, PERFECTION
KAMAL AL HOUSN	الحسن	KAH-MAHL-AHL-HOOSN	PERFECTION IN BEAUTY
KAMAR	قمر	KAH-MAHR	MOON
KAMEL	كامل	KAH-MEL	ENTIRE, COMPLETE
KAMEL AL AWSAF	الاوصاف	KAH-MEL-AHL-AHW-SAHF	THE PERFECT DESCRIPTION
KAMSEEN	خمسين	KAHM-SEEN	SANDSTORM
KARAMAH	كرامة	KAH-RAH-MAH	GRACIOUSNESS
KARAZ	كرز	KAH-RAHZ	CHERRY, CHERRY TREE
KARBOUJ	كربوج	KAHR-BOOJ	CUTE
KAREEM	كريم	KAH-REEM	NOBLE, LIBERAL, GIVER
KARIM	كريم	KAH-REEM	GIVER, KIND, NOBLE
KASR	قصر	KAHSER	CASTLE

Mouhra (Filly)

ARABIC		PRONUNCIATION	TRANSLATION
		– K –	
KASM	كسم	KAHSM	FASHION STYLE, MODE
KASSARAT AL QUALB	القلب	KAH-SAH-RAHT-AHL-QUAHLB	HEART BREAKER
KASSEEYAH	قاسية	KAH-SEE-YAH	DIFFICULT
KASSLANEH	كسلانة	KAHSS-LAH-NEH	SLUGGISH, LAZY
KAWAKEB	كواكب	KAH-WAH-KEB	STARS
KAWATHER	كواثر	KAH-WAH-THER	BIRD OF PREY
KAWKABEH	كوكبة	KAW-KAH-BEH	STAR (IN THE SKY)
KAZA WAH KAZA	كزا وكزا	KAH-ZAH-WAH-KAH-ZAH	SO AND SO
KAZEM	كاظم	KAH-ZEM	SPEECHLESS
KHAFAZEH	قفازة	KAH-FAH-ZEH	JUMPER
KHAMSA	خمسة	KAHM-SAH	FIVE
KHAREEJAH	خارجة	KAH-REE-JAH	GOING OUT
KHATIRAH	خطيرة	KHAH-TEE-RAH	DANGEROUS
KHAYYALEH	خيالة	KHAY-YAH-LEH	HORSEWOMAN
KHOURYEH	خورية	KHOO-REE-YEH	PREACHER
KHUFFIYA	خفية	KHU-FEE-YAH	HEADDRESS
KIFAYA	كفاية	KEE-FAH-YAH	SUFFICIENT
KIRMALEK	كرمالك	KEER-MAH-LEHK	FOR YOU ONLY
KISLANEH WAH MAHBOUBEH	كسلانة ومحبوبة	KEES-LAH-NEH-WAH-MAH-BOO-BEH	LAZY AND LOVED
KOUBLAH	قبلة	KOU-BLAH	KISS
KOUBLAT AL ZILAL	قبلة الزلال	KOO-BLAHT-AHL-ZEE-LAHL	KISS OF THE SHADOW
KOUSOUF	كسوف	KOO-SOOF	ECLIPSE
KURDIEH	كردية	KUHR-DEE-YEH	KURDISH GIRL
KURDIYAH	كردية	KUHR-DEE-YAH	KURDISH ORIGIN

Mouher (Colt)

ARABIC		*PRONUNCIATION*	*TRANSLATION*
		– K –	
KASSAR AL ALB	كسار القلب	KAH-SSAR-AHL-AHLB	THE HEART BREAKER
KASSEE	قاسي	KAH-SEE	DIFFICULT
KASSLAN	كسلانه	KAHSS-LAN	LAZY
KATIR	خطير	KHAH-TEER	DANGEROUS
KAWKAB	كوكب	KAW-KAHB	STAR IN THE SKY
KAZA WAH KAZA	كزا وكزا	KAH-ZAH-WAH-KAH-ZAH	SO AND SO
KHAFAZ	قفاز	KAH-FAHZ	JUMPER
KHAMSA	خمسة	KAHM-SAH	FIVE
KHAREEJ	خارج	KAH-REEJ	GOING OUT
KHARIF	خريفه	KHAH-REEF	AUTUMN
KHARIF AL OUMR	العمر	KHAH-REEF-AHL-OUMR	THE AUTUMN OF MY LIFE
KHATER	خاطر	KHAH-TER	IMAGINATION
KHAYALEEN	خيالينه	KHAH-YAH-LEEN	CAVALRY
KHAYYAL	خيال	KHAY-YAHL	HORSEMAN
KHAYYAL ZAMAN	خيال زمانه	KHAY-YAHL-ZAH-MAN	HORSEMAN FOR THE AGES
KHOURY	خوري	KHOU-REE	PREACHER
KIBKAB	كبكاب	KEEB-KAHB	CLOGS
KISHTABAN	كشتبانه	KISH-TAH-BAHN	THIMBLE
KIYAN	كيانه	KEE-YAHN	EXISTENCE, NATURE
KOUBLAH	قبلة	KOO-BLAH	KISS
KOUBLAT AL ZILAL	الزلال	KOO-BLAHT-AHL-ZEE-LAHL	KISS OF THE SHADOW
KOUTRAN	قطرانه	KOO-TRAN	PINE TAR
KURDAN	كردانه	KUHR-DAHN	NECK CHAIN
KURDI	كردي	KUHR-DEE	KURDISH ORIGIN

Mouhra (Filly)

ARABIC		PRONUNCIATION	TRANSLATION
	– L –		
LABEESSAH	لابسة	LAH-BEE-SAH	DRESSED
LABIBAH	لبيبة	LAH-BEE-BAH	SMART, INTELLIGENT
LAHBAT	لهبة	LAH-BAHT	FLAME
LAHFANEH	لهفانة	LAH-FAH-NEH	GRIEVED
LAHHABEH	لهابة	LAH-HAH-BEH	TO BE INFATUATED WITH
LAHIQUAH	لاحقة	LAH-HEE-QUAH	FOLLOWER
LAHJAT	لهجة	LAH-JAHT	TONE OF VOICE
LAMHAT	لمحة	LAHM-HAHT	GLANCE, EYE-CATCHING
LATAFAT	لطافة	LAH-TAH-FAHT	REFINEMENT
LATIFAH	لطيفة	LAH-TEE-FAH	GRACEFUL, KIND
LATMAH	لطمة	LAHT-MAH	SLAP ON THE FACE
LAWAZEM	لوازم	LAH-WAH-ZEM	DUTY
LAWMA	لومة	LAW-MAH	WERE IT NOT FOR
LAYEEQAH	لائقة	LAH-YEE-KAH	DECENT
LAYEHAT	لائحة	LAH-YEH-HAHT	SCHEDULE
LAYYENAH	لينة	LAH-YEH-NAH	SOFT
LAZEEZAH	لزيزة	LAH-ZEE-ZAH	DELIGHTFUL
LAZIZA	لزيزة	LAH-ZEE-ZAH	SWEET, PLEASANT
LEILAH	ليلة	LEH-LAH	NIGHT
LEILAT	ليلة	LEH-LAHT	MANY NIGHTS
LEYLEH	ليلة	LEH-LEH	EVENING
LEYMOONEH	ليمونة	LEH-MOON-NEH	LEMON
LOULOU	لولو	LOO-LOO	PEARL
LOUYOUNEH	لويونة	LOUH-YOO-NEH	SOFTNESS

Mouher (Colt)

ARABIC		PRONUNCIATION	TRANSLATION
		– L –	
LABESS	لابس	LAH-BESS	DRESSED
LABIB	لبيب	LAH-BEEB	INTELLIGENT
LAFEEF	لفيفة	LAH-FEEF	MIXED CROWD
LAHAWEE	لهاوي	LAH-HAH-WEE	PALATIAL
LAHEEB	لهيب	LAH-HEEB	FLAME, BLAZE
LAHFAN	لهفانة	LAH-FAHN	GRIEVED
LAHIQ	لاحقة	LAH-HIQ	FOLLOWER
LAHOOTEE	لاهوتي	LAH-HOO-TEE	THEOLOGIAN
LAMAAN	لمعانة	LAH-MAHN	FLASH, BRIGHTNESS
LAMEES	لاميس	LAH-MEES	TO TOUCH
LAMEH	لامح	LAH-MEH	GLEAMING, SHINING
LAMLAM	لملم	LAHM-LAHM	TO GATHER (AS A GROUP)
LATIF	لطيف	LAH-TEEF	GENTLE, KIND
LAWAZEM	لوازم	LAH-WAH-ZEM	DUTY
LAWWA	لوا	LAH-WAH	TO BEND
LAYEQ	لائقة	LAH-YEK	DECENT
LAYYIN	لاينة	LAH-YEN	SOFT
LAZEEZ	لزيز	LAH-ZEEZ	DELIGHTFUL
LAZEEZ AL ALWAN	لزيز الالوانة	LAH-ZEEZ-AHL-AHL-WAHN	THE DELIGHTFUL COLORS
LAZEM	لازم	LAH-ZEM	NECESSARY
LAZIZ	لزيز	LAH-ZEEZ	SWEET, PLEASANT
LEEMAZA	ليمازة	LEE-MAH-ZAH	WHY?
LEIL	ليل	LAY-IL	NIGHT
LOWN	لونة	LOUN	COLOR

Mouhra (Filly)

ARABIC		PRONUNCIATION	TRANSLATION
– L –			
LOWLABEE	لولبية	LOW-LAH-BEE	SPIRAL
LOWM	لومة	LAUM	BLAME, CENSURE
LULU	لولو	LOO-LOO	PEARL
LULU AL ABYAD	لولو الابيض	LOO-LOO-AHL-AHB-YAHD	THE WHITE PEARL
– M –			
MA AJMALA	ما أجمله	MAH-AJ-MAH-LAH	HOW BEAUTIFUL
MAAROUFAH	معروفة	MAH-ROO-FAH	WELL KNOWN
MADINAT AL SALAM	مدينة	MAH-DEE-NAT-AHL-SAH-LAHM	THE CITY OF PEACE, BAGDAD
MAGFOURAH	مغفورة	MAHG-FOO-RAH	FORGIVEN ONE
MAHBOUBEH	محبوبة	MAH-BOO-BEH	SPECIAL ONE, LOVED ONE
MAHEERAH	ماهرة	MAH-HEE-RAH	SKILLFUL
MAHFOUZAH	محفوظة	MAH-FOO-ZAH	ONE THAT YOU KEEP, KEPT
MAHROUSSEH	محروسة	MAH-ROO-SSEH	PROTECTED ONE (BY GOD)
MAJEEDAH	ماجدة	MAH-JEE-DAH	NOBLE, GLORIOUS
MAJHOOLAH	مجهولة	MAJ-HOO-LAH	PASSIVE
MAJNOUNEH	مجنونة	MAHJ-NOO-NEH	SPUNKY, LIVELY, CRAZY
MAKTOUMAH	مكتومة	MAHK-TOO-MAH	CLANDESTINE
MALAHAT	ملاحة	MAH-LAH-HAT	BEAUTY, GODLINESS
MALAKEH	ملاكة	MAH-LAH-KEH	ANGEL
MALALAT	ملالت	MAH-LAH-LAHT	WEARINESS
MALEEKAH	ماليكة	MAH-LEE-KAH	OWNER
MALIKAH	ماليكة	MA-LEE-KAH	QUEEN, RULER
MALOUNEH	ملعونة	MAH-LOO-NEH	SASSY

ARABIC		PRONUNCIATION	TRANSLATION

– L –

LOWZ	لوز	LOWZ	ALMOND
LULU	لولو	LOO-LOO	PEARL
LUZOUM	لوزوم	LUH-ZOOM	NECESSITY

– M –

MAAROUF	معروف	MAH-ROOF	WELL KNOWN
MAGFOUR	مغفور	MAHG-FOOR	FORGIVEN ONE
MAHBOUB	محبوب	MAH-BOUB	SPECIAL ONE, LOVED ONE
MAHER	ماهر	MAH-HER	SKILLFUL
MAHFOUZ	محفوظ	MAH-FOOZ	KEPT, ONE THAT YOU KEEP
MAHLIK	مالك	MAH-LIK	OWNER
MAHRAJAN	مهرجانة	MAH-RAH-JAHN	PAGEANT, FEAST, CONCERT
MAHROUSS	محروس	MAH-ROOSS	PROTECTED ONE (BY GOD)
MAJEED	مجيد	MAH-JEED	NOBLE, GLORIOUS
MAJHOOL	مجهول	MAHJ-HOOL	PASSIVE
MAJNOUN	مجنونة	MAHJ-NOON	SPUNKY, LIVELY, CRAZY
MAKTOUM	مكتوم	MAHK-TOOM	CLANDESTINE
MALAK	ملاك	MAH-LAHK	ANGEL
MALIK	مالك	MA-LIK	KING, RULER
MALOUN	ملعونة	MAHL-OON	SASSY
MALTOUSH	ملطوش	MAL-TOOSH	BRAINLESS, NO COMMON SENSE
MAMDOOH	ممدوح	MAM-DOOH	PRAISED
MAMELUK	مملوك	MAH-MEH-LOOK	TO BE OWNED
MAMLAKEE	مملكة	MAM-LAH-KEE	KINGDOM, EMPIRE

Mouhra (Filly)

ARABIC		PRONUNCIATION	TRANSLATION
		– M –	
MALTOUSHAH	حلطوشة	MAL-TOO-SHAH	BRAINLESS, NO COMMON SENSE
MALYOUN	مليونه	MAL-YOON	MILLION
MAMDOOHAH	حمدوهة	MAM-DOO-HAH	PRAISED
MAMELUKAH	مملدكة	MAH-MEH-LOO-KAH	POSSESSED, OWNED
MAMNOONIEH	مأمونية	MAM-NOO-NEE-YIEH	OBLIGATION
MARAH	مرح	MAH-RAH	VERY HAPPY
MARFOUDAH	مرفودة	MAHR-FOO-DAH	REJECTED
MARHABA	مرحبة	MAR-HAH-BAH	HELLO, GREETING
MARSAT	مرساة	MAHR-SAHT	ROPE, CORD
MARZOUKAH	مرزوقة	MAHR-ZOO-KAH	BLESSED
MASHEEYAH	ماشية	MAH-SHEE-YAH	WALKING
MASHGOOLEH	مشغولة	MAHSH-GOO-LEH	BUSY
MASHOURAH	مشهورة	MASH-HOO-RAH	WIDELY KNOWN
MASJOUNEH	مسجونة	MAHS-JOO-NEH	PRISONER
MASRIYAH	مصرية	MAHS-REE-YAH	GIRL FROM EGYPT
MATLOOBEH	مطلوبة	MAHT-LOO-BEH	IN DEMAND
MATLOUBEH	مطلوبة	MAHT-LOU-BEH	WANTED, IN DEMAND
MATROUKAH	متروكة	MAH-TROO-KAH	ABANDONED
MAULOODAH	مولودة	MAHW-LOO-DAH	BORN
MAWAHEB	مواحب	MAH-WAH-HEB	INSPIRATION
MAWLUDAH BAKEER	بكير	MAHW-LOO-DAH-BAH-KEER	BORN EARLY
MEELADAH	ميلادة	MEE-LAH-DAH	BIRTH
MEHDIEH	مهدية	MEH-DEE-YEH	GUIDED
MEHMIYEH	حمية	MEH-MEE-YEH	PROTECTED

93

Mouher (Colt)

ARABIC		PRONUNCIATION	TRANSLATION
		– M –	
MARAH	حرح	MAH-RAH	HAPPINESS
MARFOUD	حرفوض	MAHR-FOOD	REJECTED
MARHABA	حرحبة	MAR-HAH-BAH	HELLO, GREETING
MARID	حاريد	MAH-REED	REBELLIOUS
MARZOUK	حرزوق	MAHR-ZOOK	BLESSED
MASHAKEL	مشاكل	MAH-SHAH-KEL	TROUBLE
MASHEE	ماشي	MAH-SHEE	WALKING
MASJOUN	مسجونه	MAHS-JOON	PRISONER
MASR	مصر	MAHSER	EGYPT
MASRI	مصري	MAHS-REE	EGYPTIAN
MATLOUB	مطلوب	MAHT-LOOB	WANTED
MATROUK	متروكه	MAH-TROOK	ABANDONED
MATTAR	مطر	MAH-TAHR	RAIN
MAULOOD	مولود	MAHW-LOOD	BORN
MAWLUUD	مولود	MAHW-LOOD	BORN
MEELAHD	ميلاد	MEE-LAHD	BIRTH
MEHDI	مهدي	MEH-DEE	GUIDED ONE
MERJAN	حرجانه	MEHR-JAHN	CORAL
MEYDAN	ميدانه	MEH-DAHN	ARENA, SQUARE
MISHKALJEE	مشكلجي	MISH-KAHL-JEE	TROUBLE MAKER
MISK	مسك	MEESK	MUSK
MIZAJ	ميزاج	MEE-ZAHJ	TEMPERAMENT
MOOARADAT	موارادات	MOO-AHR-AH-DAHT	DEFIANCE
MOOHAREK	موحركه	MOO-HAH-REK	AGITATOR

Mouhra (Filly)

ARABIC		PRONUNCIATION	TRANSLATION
		– M –	
MERAYAT	ميدايت	MEE-RAH-YAHT	MIRROR
MERJANEH	مرجانة	MEHR-JAH-NEH	CORAL
MERTAHAH	مرتاحة	MER-TAH-HAH	RESTED
MESHMESHAH	مشمشة	MESH-MEH-SHAH	APRICOT
MINHAT	منحة	MIN-HAHT	GIFT, FAVOR
MISHKALJIYAH	مشكلجية	MISH-KHAHL-JEE-YAH	TROUBLE MAKER
MONIET	منية	MOO-NIET	WISH
MONIET AL NEFOUS	منية النفوس	MOO-NIET-AHL-NOO-FOOS	WISH OF THE SOUL
MOOHAREEKAH	محركة	MOO-HAH-REE-KAH	AGITATOR
MOONIRAH	منيرة	MOO-NEE-RAH	BRIGHT
MOOTAFAREEDAH	متفردة	MOO-TAH-FAH-REE-DAH	ALONE
MOUBARAKEH	مباركة	MOO-BAH-RAH-KEH	BLESSED ONE
MOUDAFEAH	مدافعة	MOO-DAH-FEH-AH	DEFENDER
MOUDEERAH	مديرة	MOO-DEE-RAH	LEADER
MOUFATESHAH	مفتشة	MOO-FAH-TESH-AH	SEEKER, SEARCHING FOR SOMETHING
MOUFTAKERAH	مفتخرة	MOOF-TAH-KEH-RAH	TRIUMPHANT
MOUHAJABEH	محجبة	MOO-HAH-JAH-BEH	VEILED
MOUHEBAH	موهبة	MOO-HEH-BAH	PASSIONATE
MOUHIBAH	محبة	MOO-HEE-BAH	LOVING, AFFECTIONATE
MOUHJAT	مهجة	MOO-JAHT	SOUL, LIFE
MOUHRA	مهرة	MOOH-RAH	FILLY
MOUHRA HELWEH	مهرة حلوة	MOOH-RAH-HEL-WEH	BEAUTIFUL FILLY
MOUJAWIRAH	مجاورة	MOU-JAH-WEE-RAH	NEXT DOOR NEIGHBOR
MOUMASSILAH	ممثلة	MOO-MAHS-SEE-LAH	ACTOR

Mouher (Colt)

ARABIC		PRONUNCIATION	TRANSLATION
	– M –		
MORAFIC	حرافقه	MOO-RAH-FEK	ROAD COMPANION
MOUAZAR	مودزار	MOO-AH-ZAHR	MAJESTIC
MOUBARAK	موبارك	MOO-BAH-RACK	BLESSED ONE
MOUBASHER	موبثد	MOO-BAH-SHER	ANNOUNCER OF NEWS
MOUDAFEH	مودامع	MOO-DAH-FEH	DEFENDER
MOUDEER	موديد	MOO-DEER	LEADER
MOUFATESH	موفتش	MOO-FAH-TESH	SEEKER, SEARCHING FOR SOMETHING
MOUFTAKER	مفتخر	MOOF-TAH-KEHR	TRIUMPHANT
MOUFTI	مورنى	MOOF-TEE	HOLY MAN
MOUHEB	محب	MOO-HEB	PASSIONATE
MOUHER	مهر	MOO-HER	COLT
MOUJAWER	موجاور	MOU-JAH-WER	NEXT DOOR NEIGHBOR
MOUKLIS	موخلس	MOOK-LEESS	DEVOTED
MOULAWAN	ولوته	MOO-LAH-WAHN	COLORFUL
MOUMASSEL	مومسل	MOO-MAH-SSEL	ACTOR
MOUNADEL	مونامل	MOO-NAH-DEL	ADVOCATE
MOUNAFES	موناهس	MOO-NAH-FESS	RIVAL
MOUNAWAR	مونقر	MOO-NAH-WAHR	ILLUMINATED
MOUSAFER	موسافر	MOO-SAH-FER	TRAVELER
MOUSAYTAR	موسيطو	MOO-SIGH-TAHR	DOMINANT ONE
MOUSHTAHER	موشتهر	MOOSH-TAH-HEHR	ONE OF SIGNIFICANCE, FAMOUS
MOUSHWAR	مشوار	MOOSH-WAHR	JOURNEY
MOUSSAMEH	موسامع	MOO-SSAH-MEH	ONE WHO FORGIVE
MOUSSAYTER	موسيطر	MOO-SAY-TER	HAVE THE UPPER HAND

Mouhra (Filly)

ARABIC	PRONUNCIATION	TRANSLATION

– M –

MOUNADEELAH	دوناظلة	MOO-NAH-DEE-LAH	ADVOCATE
MOUNAWARAH	دونندة	MOO-NAH-WAH-RAH	ILLUMINATED
MOUNJER	منجى	MOON-JER	FORTELLER OF THE FUTURE
MOUSAFEERAH	مونافرة	MOO-SAH-FEE-RAH	TRAVELER
MOUSHTAHERAH	متشهرة	MOOSH-TAH-HEHR-AH	SIGNIFICANT, FAMOUS
MOUSHTAHIRAH	مشتهرة	MOOSH-TAH-HEE-RAH	RENOWNED
MOUSHWAR	مشوار	MOOSH-WAHR	JOURNEY
MOUSSAMEHAH	وسامحة	MOO-SSAH-MEH-HAH	ONE WHO FORGIVES
MOUSSAYTIRAH	مسيطرة	MOO-SAY-TEE-RAH	HAVE THE UPPER HAND
MOUTAKABERAH	متكبرة	MOO-TAH-KAH-BEH-RAH	CONCEITED, SELF ASSURED
MOUTAMAYEZAH	متميزة	MOO-TAH-MAH-YEH-ZAH	PRIVILEDGE
MOUTAWAJEH	ومتوجة	MOU-TAH-WAH-JEH	CROWNED
MOUTAYASIRAH	متيسرة	MOO-TAH-YAH-SEE-RAH	WELL-OFF
MUHTARAH	محتارة	MUH-TAH-RAH	SURPRISED
MUJARADEH	مجردة	MOO-JAH-RAH-DEH	ABSTRACT, DRAWS ATTENTION AWAY FROM
MUKLEESSAH	مخلصة	MOO-KLEE-SSAH	DEVOTED
MURMUR	رخر	MUHR-MUHR	MARBLE

– N –

NABAWIAH	نباوية	NAH-BAH-WEE-YAH	PROPHETIC
NABILA	نبيلة	NAH-BEE-LAH	HIGHLY INTELLIGENT
NADA	ندا	NAH-DAH	MOISTURE, DEW
NADAMAT	ندامت	NAH-DAH-MAHT	REGRET, REPENTENCE

Mouher (Colt)

ARABIC		PRONUNCIATION	TRANSLATION
	– M –		
MOUSTAKBEL	مستقبل	MOOS-TAHK-BELL	FUTURE
MOUTAKABER	متكبر	MOO-TAH-KAH-BER	CONCEITED, SELF ASSURED
MOUTAMAYEZ	متمايز	MOO-TAH-MAH-YEZ	PRIVILEDGE
MOUTARJEM	مترجم	MOO-TAHR-JEHM	TRANSLATOR
MOUTAWAJ	متوج	MOU-TAH-WAHJ	CROWNED
MOUTAYASSIR	متيسر	MOO-TAH-YAH-SER	WELL-OFF
MOWAHAB	مواهب	MOO-WAH-HAB	INSPIRED
MUHTAR	محتار	MUH-TAHR	SURPRISED
MUJARRAD	مجرد	MOO-JAH-RAD	ABSTRACT, DRAWS ATTENTION AWAY FROM
MUJAZAT	مجازات	MOO-JAH-ZAHT	PRIZE
MUNIR	منير	MOO-NEER	BRIGHT
MURMUR	رمرم	MUHR-MUHR	MARBLE
MUTAFARRED	متفرد	MOO-TAH-FAH-RED	ALONE
	– N–		
NABAWEE	نباوية	NAH-BAH-WEE	PROPHETIC
NABIL	نبيل	NAH-BEEL	HIGHLY INTELLIGENT
NADDAF	نذافة	NAH-DAF	WOODCARVER
NADEB	نديب	NAH-DEB	WEEPER, LAMENTER
NADEEM	نديم	NAH-DEEM	CLOSE FRIEND
NADEM	نادم	NAH-DEM	PENITENT
NADER	نادر	NAH-DER	SPECIAL, UNIQUE
NADER AL JAMAL	نادر الجمال	NAH-DER-AHL-JAH-MAHL	THE RARE BEAUTY
NADIM	نديم	NAH-DEEM	INTIMATE

Mouhra (Filly)

ARABIC		PRONUNCIATION	TRANSLATION
		– N –	
NADBAT	ندبة	NAHD-BAT	SCAR
NADEEMAH	نديمة	NAH-DEE-MAH	CLOSE FRIEND
NADEERAH	نديرة	NAH-DEE-RAH	SPECIAL, UNIQUE
NADIBAH	نديبة	NAH-DEE-BAH	WEEPER, LAMENTER
NADIMAH	نادمة	NAH-DEE-MAH	INTIMATE
NADIRAH	نديرة	NAH-DEE-RAH	ONE OF A KIND, RARE
NADIRAH AL JAMEELAH	الجميلة	NAH-DEE-RAH-AHL-JAH-MEE-LAH	THE ONE OF RARE BEAUTY
NAFSANIYAH	نفسانية	NAF-SAH-NEE-YAH	FROM THE HEART
NAHDEEMAH	نادمة	NAH-DEE-MAH	PENITENT
NAHEEFAH	نا حيفة	NAH-HEE-FAH	FRAGILE, LEAN
NAHFOORAH	نافورة	NAH-FOO-RAH	WATERJET
NAHHABEH	نهابة	NAH-HAH-BEH	THIEF
NAHIFAH	نحيفة	NAH-HEE-FAH	TENDER TO THE TOUCH, LEAN
NAHLAT	نحلة	NAH-LAHT	BEE
NAHSIBAH	نصيبة	NAH-SEE-BAH	FATE
NAHZEEFAH	نظيفة	NAH-ZEE-FAH	PURE, CLEAN
NAJIHAH	ناجحة	NAH-JEE-HAH	SUCCESS
NAKHAT	نكهة	NAHK-HAHT	FRESH BREATH
NARGILEH	نركيلة	NAHR-JEE-LEH	WATER PIPE
NASABEH	نصابة	NAH-SAH-BEH	SWINDLER, THIEF
NASABEH WAH MAHBOUBEH	محبوبة	NAH-SAH-BEH-WAH-MAH-BOO-BEH	THE BELOVED THIEF
NASEEBAH	نا سبة	NAH-SEE-BAH	KINDRED
NASEEHAH	نصيحة	NAH-SEE-HAH	ADVICE, WORD TO THE WISE
NASHEEDAT	ناشدات	NAH-SHEE-DAHT	POEM, SONG

Mouher (Colt)

– N –

ARABIC		PRONUNCIATION	TRANSLATION
NADIR	نادر	NAH-DEER	ONE OF A KIND, RARE ONE
NAFOURAH	نافورة	NAH-FOOR-AH	WATER JET
NAFSANI	نفساني	NAF-SAH-NEE	FROM THE HEART
NAHAR	نهار	NAH-HAHR	DAY
NAHAWEE	نحاوي	NAH-HAH-WEE	GRAMMATICAL
NAHEEF	نحيف	NAH-HEEF	FRAGILE, LEAN
NAHHAB	نهاب	NAH-HAB	THIEF, SWINDLER
NAHIF	ناحية	NAH-HEEF	TENDER
NAHR	نهر	NAHER	RIVER
NAHZEEF	نازية	NAH-ZEEF	PURE, CLEAN
NAJAH	نجاح	NAH-JAH	SUCCESS
NAJEE	ناجي	NAH-JEE	TO CONFIDE A SECRET TO
NASEEB	نصيب	NAH-SEEB	DESTINY, FATE
NASEEM	نسيم	NAH-SEEM	SOFT BREEZE
NASEK	ناسك	NAH-SEK	HERMIT
NASHEED	ناشيد	NAH-SHEED	SONG
NASHEET	ناشط	NAH-SHEET	EAGER, FULL OF ENERGY
NASIB	نسيب	NAH-SEEB	KINDRED, RELATIVE
NASIM	نسيم	NAH-SEEM	BREEZE
NASR	نصر	NAHSR	VICTORY
NASSAB	نصاب	NAH-SAB	SWINDLER, THIEF
NASSAB AL JAMEEL	الجميل	NAH-SAB-AHL-JAH-MEEL	THE PRETTY THIEF
NASSEEHA	نصيحة	NAH-SEE-HAH	ADVICE
NASSER	ناصر	NAH-SER	CONQUERER

Mouhra (Filly)

ARABIC		PRONUNCIATION	TRANSLATION
	– N –		
NASHEETAH	نشيطة	NAH-SHEE-TAH	ACTIVE, ENERGETIC, EAGER
NASHEETAH WE HELWAH	حلوة	NAH-SHEE-TAH-WEH-HEL-WAH	BEAUTIFUL AND A BUNDLE OF ENERGY
NASIBAH	نسيبة	NAH-SEE-BAH	KIN, RELATIVE
NASIHAH	نصيحة	NAH-SEE-HAH	GUIDANCE, DIRECTION
NASIRAH	ناصرة	NAH-SEE-RAH	CONQUEROR
NASMAT	نسمة	NAHS-MAHT	BREATH OF LIFE
NASSIAT	ناصية	NAHS-SEE-YAHT	FORELOCK
NATOURAH	ناطورة	NAH-TOO-RAH	GROUNDS KEEPER, GUARD
NATOURAT ALBEE	ناطورة قلبي	NAH-TOO-RAHT-AHL-BEE	GUARDIAN OF MY HEART
NAWAFEER	نوافير	NAH-WAH-FEER	FOUNTAINS
NAYEEBAH	نايبة	NAH-YEE-BAH	DEPUTY
NAZEEKAH	نازيكة	NAH-ZEE-KAH	DELICATE
NAZEELAH	نزيلة	NAH-ZEE-LAH	LONG TERM GUEST
NAZEERAH	نظيرة	NAH-ZEE-RAH	INSPECTOR
NAZRAT	نظرة	NAHZ-RAHT	GLANCE, EYE-CATCHING
NEGM	نجم	NEHGM	STAR
NEGMAH AL SHASHA	نجمة الشاشة	NEHG-MAH-AHL-SHAH-SHAH	THE STAR OF THE SCREEN, MOVIE STAR
NEMRAH	نمرة	NEM-RAH	TIGRESS
NIHAYAT	نهاية	NEE-HAH-YAHT	END, UTMOST POINT
NIMRAH BAIDAH	نمرة بيضة	NEEM-RAH-BAHY-DAH	WHITE TIGRESS
NOOR AL NOUFOUS	نور النفوس	NOOR-AHL-NOO-FOOS	THE LIGHT OF THE SOUL
NOORIYAH	نورية	NOO-REE-YAH	DESERT PERSON
NOUFOUS	نفوس	NOO-FOOS	SOUL OF THE HEART
NOUR AL OYOUN	نور العيون	NOOR-AH-OO-YOON	LIGHT OF THE EYES

ARABIC		PRONUNCIATION	TRANSLATION
		– N –	
NASSER AL DEEN	نا صر الدين	NAH-SER-AHL-DEEN	CONQUERER OF THE FAITH
NASSIBAK	نصيبك	NAS-SEE-BAK	YOUR SHARE
NATOUR	نا طور	NAH-TOOR	GUARD, GROUNDS KEEPER
NAWAFIR	نوافير	NAH-WAH-FEER	FOUNTAINS
NAWAFIR AL HAWAH	نوافير الهوى	NAH-WAH-FEER-AHL-HAH-WAH	THE FOUNTAIN OF LOVE
NAYEB	نايب	NAH-YEB	DEPUTY
NAZEEL	نزيل	NAH-ZEEL	GUEST
NAZER	ناظر	NAH-ZER	INSPECTOR
NAZIK	ناظيك	NAH-ZEEK	DELICATE
NAZRAT	نظرة	NAHZ-RAHT	GLANCE, A QUICK LOOK
NEGM	نجم	NEHGM	STAR
NEGM AL SAHRAH	نجمة الصحراء	NEHGM-AHL-SAH-RAH	THE DESERT STAR
NEGM AL SHASHA	نجمة الشاشة	NEHGM-AHL-SHAH-SHAH	MOVIE STAR, STAR OF THE SCREEN
NIL	نيل	NEEL	NILE
NIMR	نمر	NIMR	TIGER
NIMR ABYAD	نمر ابيض	NIMR-AHB-YAHD	WHITE TIGER
NISR	نسر	NEESR	EAGLE
NISR AL AALEE	نسر العالي	NEESR-AHL-AH-LEE	THE HIGH EAGLE
NOOR AL NOUFOUS	نور النفوس	NOOR -AHL- NOO-FOOS	LIGHT OF THE SOUL
NOORI	نوري	NOO-REE	BEDOUIN, DESERT MAN
NOUFOUS	نفوس	NOO-FOOS	SPIRIT, SOUL
NOUR	نور	NOOR	LIGHT
NOUR HAYATI	نور حياتي	NOOR-HAH-YAH-TEE	THE LIGHT OF MY LIFE
NOUR AL OUYOUN	نور العيون	NOOR-AHL-OU-YOON	LIGHT OF THE EYES

Mouhra (Filly)

ARABIC		PRONUNCIATION	TRANSLATION
		– N –	
NOWFARAT	نوفرات	NOW-FAH-RAHT	WATER FOUNTAIN
		– Q –	
QADIRAH	قديرة	KAH-DEE-RAH	INFLUENTIAL
QAFFALEH	كفالة	KAHF-FAH-LEH	LOCKSMITH
		– R –	
RABABA	ربابة	RAH-BAH-BAH	FLUTE
RABBANIAH	ربانية	RAH-BAH-NEE-YAH	DIVINE
RABWAT	ربوة	RAB-WAHT	HILL, HEIGHT
RAFAHAT	رفاهة	RAH-FAH-HAHT	GOOD LIVING
RAFASSEH	رفاسة	RAH-FAH-SSEH	KICKER
RAFEEKAH	رفيقة	RAH-FEE-KAH	COMPANION
RAFIKAH	رفيقة	RAH-FEE-KAH	FRIEND (OF THE ROAD), TRAVELING COMPANION
RAHBAT	رهبة	RAH-BAHT	FEAR
RAHEBAH	راهبة	RAH-HEH-BAH	NUN
RAHEEBAH	راهيبا	RAH-HEE-BAH	FEARFUL, SCARY
RAHEEMEH	راحيمة	RAH-HEE-MEH	COMPASSIONATE
RAHEENAT	راهنة	RAH-HEE-NAHT	PLEDGE
RAHLAT	رحلة	RAH-LAHT	JOURNEY
RAHMAT	رحمة	RAH-MAHT	COMPASSION
RAHMAT ALEKEE	رحمة عليكي	RAH-MAHT-AH-LEH-KEE	COMPASSION FOR YOU
RAHMIYAH	رامية	RAH-MEE-YAH	THROWER
RAHNANAH	رنانة	RAH-NAH-NAH	SOUND MAKER
RAHWIYAH	راوية	RAH-WEE-YAH	NARRATOR
RAJFAT	رجفة	RAJ-FAHT	TREMBLING

Mouher (Colt)

ARABIC		PRONUNCIATION	TRANSLATION
		– Q –	
QADIR	خادر	KAH-DEER	INFLUENTIAL, POWERFUL
QAFFAL	قفال	KAHF-FAHL	LOCKSMITH
		– R –	
RAAD	رعد	RAH-EID	LIGHTNING, THUNDER
RABBANI	رباني	RAH-BAH-NEE	DIVINE
RABI	الربيع	RAH-BEE	SPRING (SEASON)
RAFED	رافد	RAH-FED	ONE WHO OBJECTS
RAFEEQ	رفيقه	RAH-FEEK	FRIEND (OF THE ROAD), TRAVELING COMPANION
RAFFAS	رفاس	RAH-FAHS	KICKER
RAFIK	رافيقه	RAH-FEEK	COMPANION
RAGUASS	رقاص	RAH-GUASS	DANCER
RAHEB	راهب	RAH-HEB	MONK
RAHEEB	راهيب	RAH-HEEB	FEARFUL, SCARY
RAHEEM	راحيم	RAH-HEEM	COMPASSIONATE
RAHMEE	رحمة	RAH-MEE	THROWER
RAHS AL BOOSTA	رئس البوسطة	RAHS-AHL-BOOS-TAH	POSTMASTER
RAHWEE	راوي	RAH-WEE	NARRATOR
RAJA	رجاء	RAH-JAH	TO HOPE
RAJAB	رجاب	RAH-JAB	SEVENTH MONTH OF MOSLEM YEAR
RAKKAS	رقاص	RAH-KAS	DANCER
RAMADAN	رمضان	RAH-MAH-DAHN	NINTH MONTH OF MOSLEM YEAR
RAMEH	رامح	RAH-MEH	LANCER
RAMIK	راميقه	RAH-MEEK	DARK OF COLOR

Mouhra (Filly)

ARABIC		PRONUNCIATION	TRANSLATION
		– R –	
RAKASSAH ANIKAH	رقصة انيقة	RAH-KAHS-SAH-AH-NEE-KAH	GRACEFUL DANCER
RAKEEZEH	راكزة	RAH-KEE-ZEH	CALM, SETTLED
RAMYAT	رمية	RAHM-YAHT	THROW
RAQUASSAH	رقاصة	RAH-KAH-SAH	DANCER
RASASSA	رصاصة	RAH-SAH-SSAH	LEAD (METAL), BULLET
RASHEEKAH	رشيقة	RAH-SHEE-KAH	SLENDER, ELEGANT FORM
RASHEEMAH	رشيمة	RAH-SHEE-MAH	CLUMSY
RASHEIKAH	رشيقة	RAH-SHEE-KAH	ELEGANT FORM, SLENDER
RASHWAT	رشوة	RASH-WAHT	BRIBE
RASOULEH	رسوله	RAH-SOU-LEH	MESSENGER
RAWDAH	روضة	RAW-DAH	MEADOW
RAWIYAH	راوية	RAH-WEE-YAH	ROMANCER
RAYAT	راية	RAH-YAHT	FLAGS
RAZANAT	رزانة	RAH-ZAH-NAHT	DIGNITY, GRAVITY
RAZEELAH	رزيلة	RAH-ZEE-LAH	BAD GIRL (PLAYFUL WAY)
REEHAN	ريحانة	REE-HAN	WAGER
REEMAD	رماد	REE-MAD	ASHES
REZKAH	رزقة	REHZ-KAH	INHERITENCE
RHEEMAH	ريما	RHEE-MAH	MORNING DEW
RHEEMAT HAYATEE	ريمة حياتي	RHEE-MAHT-HAH-YAH-TEE	THE MORNING DEW OF MY LIFE
RIFAT	رفعة	REE-FAHT	HIGH RANK
RIFKAT	رفقة	REEF-KAHT	COMPANY
RIYAH	رياح	REE-YAH	WIND
ROUHANI	روحاني	ROU-HAH-NEE	SPIRITUAL

Mouher (Colt)

ARABIC		PRONUNCIATION	TRANSLATION
	– R –		
RAML	رمل	RAH-MEL	SAND
RANEEN	رنينه	RAH-NEEN	TWANG (SOUND MAKING)
RANNAN	رنانة	RAH-NAN	SOUND MAKER
RASAN	رسنه	RAH-SAHN	HALTER
RASAS	رصاص	RAH-SAS	LEAD (METAL), BULLET
RASHEIK AL JISM	رشيقه الجسم	RAH-SHEEK-AHL-JISM	FINE BODY
RASHEEK	ارشيقه	RAH-SHEEK	SLIM, SLENDER
RASHEEM	ارشيم	RAH-SHEEM	CLUMSY
RASHID	رشيد	RAH-SHEED	FOLLOWER OF THE RIGHT WAY
RASID	راصد	RAH-SEED	BALANCE OF ACCOUNT
RASIF	راصفه	RAH-SEEF	FIRM, PAVED ROAD
RASOUL	رسول	RAH-SOOL	MESSENGER
RAZEEL	رزيل	RAH-ZEEL	BADBOY (IN A PLAYFUL WAY)
REDWAN	رضوانه	RED-WON	SATISFACTION
REEHAN	ريحانه	REE-HAN	WAGER
REZEK	رزقه	REH-ZEK	INHERITENCE
RIYAH	رياح	REE-YAH	WIND
	– S –		
SABAH	صباح	SAH-BAH	MORNING
SABEEL	سبيل	SAH-BEEL	ROAD
SABI	صبي	SAH-BEE	JUVENILE
SABIL	سبيل	SAH-BEEL	STREET
SABIL AL HAWAH	سبيل الهوى	SAH-BEEL-AHL-HAH-WAH	STREET OF LOVE

Mouhra (Filly)

ARABIC		PRONUNCIATION	TRANSLATION

– S –

ARABIC		PRONUNCIATION	TRANSLATION
SAADAT	حسعادات	SAH-AH-DAT	HAPPINESS
SABABA	حبابة	SAH-BAH-BAH	EXCESSIVE LOVE
SABAHAT	حباحات	SAH-BAH-HAHT	MORNINGS
SABEEYAT	حبية	SAH-BEE-YAHT	JUVENILE
SABIHAH	حبيحة	SAH-BEE-HAH	IN THE MORNING
SABIRAH	حبيرة	SAH-BEE-RAH	PATIENCE (TO HAVE)
SABIYAH	حبية	SAH-BEE-YAH	JUVENILE
SABIYEH	حبية	SAH-BEE-YEH	YOUNG WOMAN
SABWAT	حبوات	SAB-WAHT	YOUNG, YOUTHFUL
SADAH	حدا	SAH-DAH	ECHO
SADAKAT	حداقات	SAH-DAH-KAHT	TRUE FRIENDSHIP
SADEEKAT AL HAYAT	حديقةلحياة	SAH-DEE-KAHT-AHL-HAH-YAT	TRUE FRIEND FOR LIFE
SADFAT	حدفة	SAHD-FAHT	CHANCE
SADIKAH	حديقة	SAH-DEE-KAH	TRUTHFUL
SADMAT	حمة	SAHD-MAHT	SHOCK
SAFEERAH	سفيرة	SAH-FEE-RAH	AMBASSADOR
SAFRAH	حفرة	SAHF-RAH	YELLOW
SAHRA	سيرة	SAH-RAH	DESERT
SAHRANEH	سيرانة	SAH-RAH-NEH	AWAKE
SAIFEEYEH	حيفية	SAHY-FEE-YEH	SUMMER
SAJEENA	سجينة	SAH-JEE-NAH	PRISONER
SAJIDAH	ساجدة	SAH-JEE-DAH	WORSHIPPER
SAJINAH HAYATI	سجينة حياتي	SAH-JEE-NAH-HAH-YAH-TEE	PRISONER OF MY LIFE
SAKEETAH	ساكتة	SAH-KEE-TAH	SOFT SPOKEN, QUIET

ARABIC		PRONUNCIATION	TRANSLATION
		– S –	
SABIR	صابر	SAH-BEER	PATIENCE (HAVING)
SABR	صبر	SAHBER	PATIENT
SADA	صدا	SAH-DAH	ECHO
SADEEK	صادقة	SAH-DEEK	TRUE FRIEND
SADEK	صادقة	SAH-DEK	TRUTHFUL
SAFEER	سفير	SAH-FEER	AMBASSADOR
SAFI	صافى	SAH-FEE	CLEAR
SAFI AL OUYOUN	صافى العيونه	SAH-FEE-AHL-OU-YOON	THE CLEAR EYED ONE
SAHER	ساحر	SAH-HEHR	MAGICIAN
SAHRAN	سهرانه	SAH-RAHN	AWAKE
SAJEED	ساجد	SAH-JEED	WORSHIPPER
SAJEEN	سجين	SAH-JEEN	IMPRISONED
SAJIN ALBEE	سجين قلبى	SAH-JEEN-AL-BEE	PRISONER OF MY HEART
SAJIN HAYATI	سجين حياتى	SAH-JEEN-HAH-YAH-TEE	PRISONER OF MY LIFE
SAKR	صقر	SAHKR	EAGLE
SAKRAN	سكرانه	SAHK-RAHN	INTOXICATED
SALAM	سلام	SAH-LAHM	PEACE
SALAM MAAKOUM	سلام عليكم	SAH-LAHM-MAAH-KOUHM	PEACE BE WITH YOU
SALAMAT	سلامت	SAH-LAH-MAHT	GREETINGS
SALEEM	سليم	SAH-LEEM	PEACEFUL, SAFE
SALEH	صالح	SAH-LEH	GENUINE, TRUE, VIRTUOUS
SALIM	ساليم	SAH-LEEM	SAFE, PEACEFUL
SAMAH	سماح	SAH-MAH	HEAVEN
SAMAWEE	سماوى	SAH-MAH-WEE	ANGELIC

Mouhra (Filly)

ARABIC		PRONUNCIATION	TRANSLATION
		– S –	
SAKRANEH	دكرانة	SAHK-RAH-NEH	INTOXICATED
SALAMAT	سلامات	SAH-LAH-MAHT	GREETINGS, PEACE TO YOU
SALAMEH	سلامة	SAH-LAH-MEH	HELLO (SALUTATION), PEACE TO YOU
SALEEHAH	صالحة	SAH-LEE-HAH	GENUINE, SOUND, VIRTUOUS
SALEEMAH	سليمة	SAH-LEE-MAH	HEALTHY, WELL
SALIMAH	سالمة	SAH-LEE-MAH	SAFE, FREE FROM DANGER
SALIMAH MIN ALLAH	من الله	SAH-LEE-MAH-MIN-AHL-LAH	SAVED BY THE GRACE OF GOD
SALIMEH	سالمة	SAH-LEE-MEH	PEACEFUL, SAFE
SALWAT	سلوات	SAHL-WAHT	DIVERSION
SAMAH	سماح	SAH-MAH	HEAVEN
SAMAHAT	سماحة	SAH-MAH-HAHT	KINDNESS, GRACE
SAMAWEEYEH	سماوية	SAH-MAH-WEE-YEH	HEAVENLY
SAMAWHIYAH	سماوية	SAH-MAH-WEE-YAH	ANGELIC
SAMRAH	سمرة	SAHM-RAH	BROWNISH COLOR
SAMRAH WI HELWEH	وحلوة	SAHM-RAH-WEH-HELWEH	DARK AND PRETTY
SANNAT	صنعة	SAHN-AHT	WORK, CRAFT
SARAB	سراب	SAH-RAB	MIRAGE
SARIHAH	صريحة	SAH-REE-HAH	HONEST, CLEAR
SAWDAH	سودة	SAHW-DAH	BLACK ONE
SAYADDAH	صيادة	SAH-YAH-DAH	HUNTER
SEMSARAH	سمسارة	SEM-SAH-RAH	SALESWOMAN
SHABEEHAH	شابيهة	SHA-BEE-HAH	SUSPECT
SHABHAH	شبهة	SHAB-HAH	GRAY COLOR
SHADAHYED	شدايد	SHAH-DAH-YED	TRIBULATION

Mouher (Colt)

ARABIC		PRONUNCIATION	TRANSLATION
		– S –	
SARIH	صارح	SAH-REEH	HONEST, CLEAR
SAUD	صعود	SAH-OOD	CLIMB
SAWLAJAN	صولجانه	SAW-LAH-JAN	SCEPTOR
SAYADD	صياد	SAH-YAHD	HUNTER
SEIF	سيفه	SAYF	SWORD
SEMSAR	سمسار	SEM-SAHR	SALESMAN
SHAABAN	شعبانه	SHAH-BAN	EIGHTH LUNAR MONTH
SHABAB	شباب	SHAH-BAHB	YOUNG MALE
SHABEEH	شبيه	SHAH-BEAH	SUSPECT
SHADAT	شهادة	SHAH-DAT	TRIBULATION
SHADEED	شديد	SHAH-DEED	VIOLENT, STRONG
SHAFFAHF	شفافه	SHAH-FAHF	TRANSPARENT
SHAH	شاه	SHAH	IRANIAN KING
SHAHEED	شاهد	SHAH-HEED	MARTYR
SHAHEEN	شاهين	SHAH-HEEN	WHITE FALCON
SHAHEER	شاهر	SHAH-HEER	NOTORIOUS
SHAHJIH	شاجع	SHAH-JEE	BRAVE
SHAHKER	شاكر	SHAH-KEHR	GRATEFUL
SHAHWAN	شريفة	SHAH-WAN	SENSUAL, PASSIONATE
SHAKK	شك	SHAHK	SUSPICION
SHAKUR	شاكر	SHAH-KOOR	THANKFUL
SHAMALEE	شمالي	SHAH-MAH-LEE	FROM THE NORTH
SHAMAS	شماس	SHAH-MAS	DEACON
SHAMEE	شامي	SHAH-MEE	FROM DAMASCUS

Mouhra (Filly)

ARABIC		PRONUNCIATION	TRANSLATION
		– S –	
SHADEEDEH	دشديدة	SHAH-DEE-DEH	STRONG, MUSCULAR
SHAFFAFEH	شفافة	SHAH-FAH-FEH	TRANSPARENT
SHAHAMAT	شهامة	SHAH-HAH-MAT	HONOR
SHAHEEDAH	شهيدة	SHAH-HEE-DAH	MARTYR
SHAHEERAH	شهيرة	SHAH-HEE-RAH	FAMOUS
SHAHWANEH	شهوانية	SHAH-WAH-NEH	SENSUAL, PASSIONATE
SHAKIMAT	شكيمة	SHAH-KEE-MAHT	MOUTH BIT
SHAKIRAH	شاكرة	SHAH-KEE-RAH	GRATEFUL
SHAKRAH	شقراء	SHAHK-RAH	SORREL COLOR
SHAKURA	شاكورة	SHAH-KOO-RAH	THANKFUL
SHAMAH	شمعة	SHAHM-AH	CANDLE
SHAMALIYAH	شمالية	SHAH-MAH-LEE-YAH	FROM THE NORTH
SHAMIEH	شامية	SHAH-MEE-YEH	FROM DAMASCUS
SHAMS	شمس	SHAHMS	SUN
SHARAB	شراب	SHAH-RAHB	DRINKS
SHARAF	شرف	SHAH-RAF	HONOR
SHARARAT	شرارات	SHAR-RAH-RAHT	SPARK
SHAREEDAH	شريدة	SHAH-REE-DAH	ROAMING, LOST
SHAREEKAH	شريكة	SHAH-REE-KAH	PARTNER
SHARIFAH	شريفة	SHAH-REE-FAH	HONORABLE, HONEST, NOBLE
SHARIRAH	شريرة	SHAH-REE-RAH	NAUGHTY, MISBEHAVING GIRL
SHARQ	شرقه	SHARK	EAST
SHARRABAT	شرابة	SHAH-RAH-BAHT	TASSEL
SHARSHARAT	شرشرة	SHAHR-SHAH-RAHT	FRINGE

Mouher (Colt)

ARABIC		PRONUNCIATION	TRANSLATION
		– S –	
SHAMS	ستمس	SHAHMS	SUN
SHARAB	شراب	SHAH-RAHB	DRINKS
SHARAF	شرفه	SHAH-RAF	HONOR
SHARED	شارد	SHAH-RED	ROAMING
SHAREEK	شاريك	SHAH-REEK	PARTNER
SHARIF	شرفة	SHAH-REEF	HONEST, NOBLE, HONORABLE
SHARRIR	شرير	SHAH-REER	BAD BOY
SHART	شرط	SHAHRT	STIPULATION, CONDITION
SHAT AL ARAB	شط العرب	SHAHT-AHL-ARAB	THE SHORE OF ARABIA
SHATAWEE	شطاوى	SHAH-TAH-WEE	PERSON WHO LIVES NEAR SEA
SHATAWI	شطاوي	SHAH-TAH-WEE	WINTERY
SHATER	شاطر	SHAH-TEHR	ASTUTE
SHEETAN	شيطانه	SHEE-TAN	EVIL, SATAN
SHEIK	شيخ	SHEEK	HOLY MAN
SHEREER	شرير	SHEH-REER	WICKED, DEVILISH
SHORTI	شرطي	SHOR-TEE	GAURDSMAN
SHOUHUUD	شهود	SHOO-HOOD	TESTIFIERS, WITNESSES
SHOUKRAN	شكرا	SHOUK-RAHN	THANK YOU
SHUHRAT AL NASSAB	الشهرة النسب	SHOOH-RAHT-AHL-NAH-SAB	FAME OF THE ORIGIN
SIHR	سحر	SEEHR	MAGIC
SINDIYAN	سنديانه	SIN-DEE-YAN	EVERGREEN
SIRAJ AL LEIL	سراج الليل	SEE-RAJ-AHL-LAYIL	NIGHTLAMP
SOMSOUM	سمسم	SOOM-SOOM	SESAME SEED
SOUBHAN ALLAH	صبحانه الله	SOOB-HAN-AHL-LAH	PRAISE BE TO GOD

112

Mouhra (Filly)

ARABIC	PRONUNCIATION	TRANSLATION
– S –		
SHATAWIYAH شتشاوية	SHAH-TAH-WEE-YAH	WINTERY
SHATEERAH شاطرة	SHAH-TEE-RAH	ASTUTE
SHAWARED شوارد	SHAH-WAH-RED	DIFFERENT, UNUSUAL
SHAYTANAT شيطانة	SHAHY-TAH-NAHT	DEVILISHNESS
SHEEMALI شمالي	SHEE-MAH-LEE	NORTHERN OR NORTHERLY
SHEETANEH شيطاني	SHEE-TAN-NEH	EVIL, SATAN
SHERIRAH شريرة	SHEH-REER-RAH	WICKED, DEVILISH
SHOUHRAH شهرة	SHOUH-RAH	FAME
SHOUHUUD شهود	SHOO-HOOD	TESTIFIERS, WITNESSES
SHOUKOUK شكوك	SHOO-KOOK	SUSPICION
SHURUT شروط	SHOO-ROOT	STIPULATIONS, CONDITIONS
SITAR الستار	SEE-TAR	VEIL WORN BY A WOMAN
SITT ست	SITT	LADY
SOUMSOUM سمسم	SOOM-SOOM	SESAME SEED
SOURAT صورة	SOO-RAHT	PICTURE, FORM
SUBHIYAH صبحية	SOUB-HEE-YAH	MORNING PERSON
SULTANAH سلطانة	SUL-TAH-NAH	QUEEN OF AN EMIRATE
SULWAN سلوانة	SOOL-WAHN	CONSOLATION
SURIAH سرية	SOO-REE-YAH	MYSTIC
– T –		
TABASHIR تباشير	TAH-BAH-SHEER	GOOD NEWS
TABBALEH طبالة	TAH-BAH-LEH	DRUM PRAYER
TABIBAH طبيبة	TAH-BEE-BAH	PHYSICIAN

ARABIC		PRONUNCIATION	TRANSLATION
	– S –		
SOURAT	صورة	SOO-RAHT	IMAGE
SUBHI	صبحي	SOUB-HEE	MORNING PERSON
SULTAN	سلطانة	SUL-TAHN	KING OF AN EMIRATE
SURRI	سري	SOOR-REE	MYSTIC
SURUR	سرور	SOU-ROO-R	JOY, PLEASE
	– T –		
TABBAL	طبال	TAH-BAL	DRUM PRAYER
TABIB	طبيب	TAH-BEEB	PHYSICIAN
TABOUR	طابور	TAH-BOOR	BATTALION
TAFIF	طفيف	TAH-FEEF	SMALL QUANTITY
TAFSEER	تفسير	TAF-SEER	ILLUSTRATION
TAHER	طاهر	TAH-HER	PURE, CLEAN
TAHER AL NAFS	طاهر النفس	TAH-HER-AHL-NAHFS	THE PURE SOUL, THE CLEAN SOUL
TAHLEEL	تحليل	TAH-LEEL	EVOLUTION
TAHYESH	طايش	TAH-YESH	MISCHIEVOUS YOUNSTER
TAIF	طايف	TAH-IF	TOWN IN SAUDI ARABIA
TAJER	تاجر	TAH-JER	MERCHANT
TAKDEEM	تقديم	TAHK-DEEM	PRESENTATION
TAKLIB	تقليب	TAHK-LEEB	REVERSAL, CHANGE OF MIND
TALAB	طلب	TAH-LAHB	QUEST
TALEB	طالب	TAH-LEB	STUDENT, SEEKER OF KNOWLEDGE
TALJ	ثلج	TAHLJ	SNOW
TAMAM	تمام	TAH-MAM	COMPLETE

Mouhra (Filly)

ARABIC		PRONUNCIATION	TRANSLATION
	– T –		
TAHARAT	طاهرات	TAH-HAH-RAHT	PURITY
TAHEERAH	طاهرة	TAH-HEE-RAH	PURE, VIRGIN
TAHIRAH AL NAFS	طاهرة النفس	TAH-HEE-RAH-AHL-NAHFS	THE PURE SOUL, THE CLEAN SOUL
TAHREER	تحرير	TAH-REER	LIBERATION, FREEDOM
TAJEERAH	تاجرة	TAH-JEE-RAH	MERCHANT
TAKDIMAH	تقدمة	TAHK-DEE-MAH	PRESENTATION
TAKLIBAH	تقليبة	TAHK-LEE-BAH	REVERSAL, CHANGE OF MIND
TALAWAT	طلاوة	TAH-LAH-WAHT	BEAUTY, GRACE
TALBAT	طلبة	TAL-BAHT	DESIRE
TALEEBAT	طالبة	TAH-LEE-BAHT	PUPIL, STUDENT
TALIBAH	طالبة	TAH-LEE-BAH	STUDENT, SEEKER OF KNOWLEDGE
TALSAM	تلسم	TAL-SAM	TALISMAN, CHARM
TAREEK	طارقة	TAH-REEK	ROAD
TARFAT	ترفة	TAR-FAHT	TWINKLING OF AN EYE
TARHAH	طرحة	TAR-HAH	VEIL WORN BY A WOMAN
TARSHAH	طرشة	TAR-SHAH	DEAF ONE
TAWAFAN	طوفانه	TAH-WAH-FAHN	FLOOD, DELUGE
TAWAZUN	توازنه	TAH-WAH-ZOON	EQUILIBRIUM
TAWBAT	توبت	TAW-BAHT	REPENTENCE
TAWILAH	طويلة	TAH-WEE-LAH	LONG LEGGED, TALL
TAWILEH	طويلة	TAH-WEE-LEH	TALL, LONG LEGGED
TAYEEBAH	طيبة	TAH-YEE-BAH	GOOD
TAYEEBAH AL NAFS	طيبة النفس	TAH-YEE-BAH-AHL-NAHFS	THE GOOD HEARTED SOUL
TAYIHAH	تيهة	TAH-YEE-HAH	LOST

Mouher (Colt)

– T –

ARABIC		PRONUNCIATION	TRANSLATION
TAMOUZ	تموز	TAH-MOOZ	JULY
TAR	طار	TAHR	REVENGE
TARAF AL EIN	طرف العين	TAH-RAHF-AHL-EIN	LID OF THE EYE, EYELID
TARBOUSH	طربوش	TAHR-BOOSH	HEADGEAR
TAREEK	طريقة	TAH-REEK	STREET
TAREEK AL HAWAH	الريق	TAH-REEK-AL-HAH-WAH	THE STREET OF LOVE
TARIK	طاريقة	TAH-REEK	ROAD
TAWAFAN	طوفانة	TAH-WAH-FAHN	FLOOD, DELUGE
TAWAFF	طوافة	TAH-WAF	LEAD AROUND
TAWASH	طواش	TAH-WASH	GELDING
TAWEEL	طويل	TAH-WEEL	TALL
TAWIL	طويل	TAH-WEEL	LONG LEGS
TAWOOS	طاووس	TAH-WOOSS	PEACOCK
TAYEB	طيب	TAH-YEB	GOOD
TAYEH	تايه	TAH-YEH	LOST
TAYEH WAH MATLOUB	ومطلوب	TAH-YEH-WAH-MAT-LOOB	LOST AND IN DEMAND
TAYYAR	طيار	TAH-YAHR	PILOT
TAYYEB AL NAFS	طيب النفس	TAH-YEB-AHL-NAHFS	THE GOOD HEARTED SOUL
TAZWEEN	تزوينه	TAHZ-WEEN	ADORNMENT
TELMIZ	تلميذ	TEL-MEEZ	ONE WHO LEARNS, STUDENT
TEMSAH	تمساح	TEM-SAH	CROCIDILE
TOUNISEE	تونيسي	TOO-NEE-SEE	FROM TOUNIS (in Middle East)
TOURJUMAN	تورجمان	TOOR-JOO-MAN	TRANSLATOR
TURKI	تركي	TUR-KEE	TURK

Mouhra (Filly)

ARABIC		PRONUNCIATION	TRANSLATION
– T –			
TAYISHAH	طائشة	TAH-YEE-SHAH	MISCHIEVIOUS YOUNSTER
TAYYAR	طيار	TAH-YAHR	PILOT
TAYYARAH	طيارة	TAH-YAH-RAH	PLANE
TAYYEB	طيب	TAH-YEB	IN GOOD HEALTH
TAYYEBAH	طيبة	TAH-YEH-BAH	GOOD HEARTED
TAZWEENAH	تزوينة	TAHZ-WEE-NAH	ADORNMENT
TEERAZ	طيراز	TEE-RAHZ	MODE, MANNER, STYLE
TEHFAT	تحفة	TEH-FAHT	CHERISHED OBJECT, GIFT
TELMIZEH	تلميذة	TIL-MEE-ZEH	ONE WHO LEARNS, STUDENT
TERSANEH	ترسانة	TER-SAH-NEH	ARSENAL
TOUNISSIYAH	تونسية	TOO-NEE-SEE-YAH	FROM TOUNIS (in Middle East)
TOURJAMANEH	ترجمانة	TOOR-JAH-MAH-NEH	TRANSLATOR
TURKIYEH	تركية	TUR-KEE-YEH	TURKISH WOMAN
– W –			
WAHEEDAH	وحيدة	WHAH-HEE-DAH	ONLY DAUGHTER
WAJAHAT	وجاهة	WAH-JAH-HAHT	CONSIDERATION, POSITION
WAJBAT	وجبة	WAHJ-BAT	SET OF SAME KIND
WAJEEHAH	وجيهة	WHAH-JEE-HAH	PRINCESS
WAJNAT	وجنة	WAHJ-NAHT	CHEEK, FACE
WAKEELAH	وكيلة	WAH-KEE-LAH	ONE WHO PLEADS A CAUSE
WAKEELAT	وكيلات	WAH-KEE-LAHT	COMMISSARIES
WAKILAT	وكيلة	WAH-KEE-LAHT	AGENT, SUBSTITUTE
WALEEYAT	ولية	WAH-LEE-YAHT	PATRON

Mouher (Colt)

ARABIC		PRONUNCIATION	TRANSLATION
		– W –	
WADI	وادي	WAH-DEE	VALLEY
WAFD	وفد	WAHFD	AN ENVOY
WAHED	واحد	WHAH-HED	ONLY ONE, UNIQUE
WAHEED	واحيد	WHAH-HEED	ONLY CHILD
WAHM	وهم	WAH-HIM	ILLUSION
WAJAL	وجال	WHAH-JAHL	TO FEAR
WAJEB	واجب	WHAH-JEB	DUTY
WAJEEH	واجيه	WHAH-JEEH	CHIEF, PRINCE
WAKEEL	واكيل	WAH-KEEL	ONE WHO PLEADS A CAUSE
WAKIL	واكل	WAH-KEEL	COMMISSARY
WALEE	والي	WAH-LEE	PATRON
WALI	دالي	WAH-LEE	CHIEF
WALI AL BEIT	والي البيت	WAH-LEE-AHL-BEIT	CHIEF OF THE HOUSE
WASEET	واسيط	WAH-SEET	MEDIATOR
WASSIK	واثقه	WAH-SEEK	RELIABLE
WASSIT	واسط	WAH-SEET	INTERMEDIARY
WATAN	وطن	WAH-TAN	COUNTRY
WATANI	وطني	WAH-TAH-NEE	FAITHFUL TO HIS COUNTRY
WAYNAK	وينك	WAY-NAHK	WHERE ARE YOU?
WAYNAK YA HELOU	ياحلو	WAY-NAHK-YAH-HEH-LOO	WHERE ARE YOU PRETTY ONE
WAZEER	وازير	WAH-ZEER	ADVISOR, MINISTER
WAZWAZA	وزوزة	WAHZ-WAH-ZAH	HUM (FROM HUMMING)
WEEDAD	ويداد	WEE-DAD	LOVE, AFFECTION
WEEDAA	ويداع	WEE-DAA	FAREWELL

Mouhra (Filly)

ARABIC		PRONUNCIATION	TRANSLATION
– W –			
WALIYAH	وليّة	WAH-LEE-YAH	CHIEF
WARDI	وردي	WAHR-DEE	ROSE COLORED
WARDI HAMRAH	وردة حمرة	WAHR-DEE-HAM-RAH	RED ROSE
WARED	وارد	WAH-RED	INCOME
WASEETAH	واسيطة	WAH-SEE-TAH	MEDIATOR
WASSIKAH	واسقة	WAH-SEE-KAH	RELIABLE
WASSITAH	واسطة	WAH-SEE-TAH	INTERMEDIARY
WASSIYAH	وصية	WAH-SEE-YAH	WILL, TESTAMENT
WATANIAH	وطنية	WAH-TAH-NEE-YAH	FAITHFUL TO ONE'S COUNTRY
WAYNEK	وَينك	WAY-NEK	WHERE ARE YOU?
WAYNEK YA HELWAH	يا حلوة	WAY-NEK-YAH-HEL-WAH	WHERE ARE YOU PRETTY ONE?
WAZIRAH	وزيرة	WAS-ZEE-RAH	MINISTER, ADVISOR
WAZNAT	وزنت	WAHZ-NAHT	WEIGHT
WAZWAZAH	وزوزة	WAZ-WAH-ZAH	HUM (FROM HUMMING)
WEEDAD	وِداد	WEE-DAD	LOVE, AFFECTION
WEEQAR	وِقار	WEE-KAHR	HIGH REGARD, RESPECT
WEHDAT	وحدة	WEH-DAHT	UNION, SOLITUDE
WOUROUD	ورود	WOO-ROOD	ROSES
– Y –			
YA BINT AL RIYAH	يا بنة الرياح	YAH-BINT-AHL-REE-YAH	OH, DAUGHTER OF THE WIND
YA HAYATI	يا حياتي	YAH-HAH-YAH-TEE	MY LIFE
YA HABIBTEE	يا حبيبتي	YAH-HAH-BEEB-TEE	OH, DARLING
YA JAMEELAH	يا جميلة	YAH-JAH-MEE-LAH	OH, BEAUTIFUL ONE

Mouher (Colt)

ARABIC		PRONUNCIATION	TRANSLATION
– W –			
WEEQAR	وقار	WEE-KAR	HIGH REGARD, RESPECT
WEESAM	حيسام	WEE-SAHM	BADGE OF HONOR
– Y –			
YA ALLAH	يالله	YAH-ALLAH	OH, GOD
YA HAYATI	يا حياتي	YAH-HAH-YAH-TEE	MY LIFE
YA JAMEEL	يا جميل	YAH-JAH-MEEL	OH, BEAUTIFUL ONE
YA ZEID	يا زيد	YAH-ZED	OH, ZEID
YABESS	يابس	YAH-BESS	DRY ONE
YADAWEE	يداوي	YAH-DAH-WEE	MANUAL
YAKEEN	ياقينة	YAH-KEEN	CONVICTION
YAKIN	ياقينة	YAH-KEEN	STRONG BELIEF
YAKOUT	ياقوت	YAH-KOOT	RUBY
YAMEEN	يامين	YAH-MEEN	OATH, TO THE RIGHT
YA-OUMEE	يا أمي	YAH-OU-MEE	OH, MOM
YASIR	ياسر	YAH-SEER	PROSPEROUS
YATIM	يتيم	YAH-TEEM	ORPHAN
YUNIS	يونس	YOO-NEES	JONAH
– Z –			
ZABARDAJ	زبردج	ZAH-BAR-DAJ	CRYSTALLITE
ZAHAWAT	زهاوة	ZAH-HAH-WAHT	VIVIDNESS
ZAHER	زاهر	ZAH-HER	EVIDENT
ZAHIR	زاهر	ZAH-HER	CLEAR, DISTINCT
ZAIM	زعيم	ZAH-EEM	LEADER, CHIEF

Mouhra (Filly)

ARABIC		PRONUNCIATION	TRANSLATION
– Y –			
YABISSAH	يابسة	YAH-BEE-SAH	DRY ONE
YAMAMAT	يامامة	YAH-MAH-MAHT	DOVE
YASIRAH	ياسرة	YAH-SEE-RAH	PROSPEROUS
YASMIN	يسمين	YAS-MEEN	JASMINE
YASSAR	يسار	YAH-SAHR	LEFT
YATEEMAH	يتيمة	YAH-TEE-MAH	ORPHAN
YATIMAH	يتيمة	YAH-TEE-MAH	ORPHAN
YATIMAH WAH HANOUNEH	حنونة	YAH-TEE-MAH-WAH-HAH-NOO-NEH	KIND AND ORPHANED
YOUSRAH	يسرة	YOUS-RAH	LEFT HANDED
YUMNAT	يومنة	YOOM-NAHT	RIGHT SIDE
– Z –			
ZAFEER	زفير	ZAH-FEER	SOUND OF WIND
ZAGLOULEH	زغلولة	ZAHG-LOO-LEH	BIRD
ZAHABIEH	زهبية	ZAH-HAH-BEE-YEH	GOLDEN
ZAHAWAT	زهاوة	ZAH-HAH-WAHT	VIVIDNESS
ZAHRAH	زهرة	ZAH-RAH	FLOWER
ZAHRAH HAMRAH	زهرة حمرة	ZAH-RAH-HAM-RAH	RED FLOWER
ZAIMAH	زاعيمة	ZAH-EE-MAH	DICTATOR
ZAIMEH	زاعيمة	ZAH-EE-MEH	LEADER
ZAIRAH	زائرة	ZAH-YEAR-AH	VISITING GUEST
ZAIRAHT ALBEE	زائرة قلبي	ZAH-YEAR-AHT-AHL-BEE	VISITING MY HEART
ZAITUNAT	زيتونة	ZAHY-TOO-NAHT	OLIVES
ZAKEEYEH	زكية	ZAH-KEE-YEH	WITTY, RESOURCEFUL

121

Mouher (Colt)

ARABIC		PRONUNCIATION	TRANSLATION
		– Z –	
ZAIR	رايير	ZAH-YEAR	GUEST
ZAITOON	زيتعنه	ZAHY-TOON	OLIVE
ZAJAL	زرجان	ZAH-JAL	UPROAR
ZAKEE	زكى	ZAH-KEE	INTELLIGENT, CLEVER
ZAKI	زكى	ZAH-KEE	WITTY, CLEVER, CUNNING
ZAKI KTEER	زكى كثير	ZAH-KEE-KTEER	OVERLY INTELLIGENT AND CUNNING
ZALEM	ظالم	ZAH-LEM	DICTATOR
ZALZAL	زلزال	ZAL-ZAL	TO SHAKE, RUMBLING
ZAMEEL	زاميل	ZAH-MEEL	FRIEND
ZAMEEL AL OUMR	زميل العمر	ZAH-MEEL-AHL-OUMR	FRIEND FOR LIFE
ZAMIL	زاميل	ZAH-MEEL	COMRADE
ZAMMAR	زمار	ZAH-MAR	PIPER
ZANBOUR	زنبور	ZAN-BOOR	HORNET
ZAYEED	زايد	ZAH-YEED	ABUNDANT
ZAYER	زاير	ZAH-YER	VISITOR
ZAYID	زايد	ZAH-YEED	PLENTIFUL
ZEENAT	زينة	ZEE-NAHT	ORNAMENT
ZEJAJ	زجاج	ZEE-JAJ	GLASS
ZILAL	زلال	ZEE-LAHL	SHADOW
ZILAL AL HAWAH	زلال الهها	ZEE-LAHL-AHL-HAH-WAH	SHADOW OF LOVE
ZILZAL	زلزال	ZIL-ZAHL	EARTHQUAKE
ZIYARAT	زيارات	ZEE-YAH-RAHT	VISITS
ZOULAL	زولال	ZOO-LAHL	CLEAR COOL PURE WATER
ZUHUR	أزهور	ZOO-HOOR	FLOWERS

Mouhra (Filly)

ARABIC		PRONUNCIATION	TRANSLATION
		– Z –	
ZAKIEH	زكية	ZAH-KEE-YEH	INTELLIGENT, CLEVER
ZAKIYAH	زكيّة	ZAH-KEE-YAH	CLEVER, CUNNING
ZALZALEH	زلزالة	ZAL-ZAH-LEH	RUMBLING, TO SHAKE
ZAMAN	زمانه	ZAH-MAN	TIME
ZAMILEH	زميلة	ZAH-MEE-LEH	COMPANION, FRIEND
ZAMILEH AL OUMR	زميلة العمر	ZAH-MEE-LAH-AHL-OUMR	THE FRIEND FOR LIFE
ZANBUK	زنبك	ZAN-BOOK	LILY, IRIS
ZARAFAT	زرافات	ZAH-RAH-FAHT	GIRAFFE
ZARIFFAH	زريفة	ZAH-REE-FAH	ELEGANT
ZARKAH	زرقة	ZAR-KAH	BLUE COLOR
ZARKAWI	زرقاوي	ZAR-KAH-WEE	BLUE-GRAY COLOR
ZAYEEDAH	زايدة	ZAH-YEE-DAH	ABUNDANT
ZAYIRAH	زايرة	ZAH-YEE-RAH	VISITOR
ZEENAT	زينة	ZEE-NAHT	ORNAMENT
ZILAL	زيلال	ZEE-LAHL	SHADOW
ZILAL ALBEE	قلبي	ZEE-LAHL-AHL-BEE	SHADOW OF MY HEART
ZILAL AL HAWAH	الهوا	ZEE-LAHL-AHL HAH-WAH	SHADOW OF LOVE
ZILZALEH	زلزالة	ZIL-ZAH-LEH	EARTHQUAKE
ZINAHT	زينة	ZEE-NAHT	DECORATION
ZIYARAT	زيارات	ZEE-YAH-RAHT	VISITS
ZUHUR	زهور	ZOO-HOOR	FLOWERS
ZUHUR WA ALWAN	والوانه	ZOO-HOOR-WAH-AHL-WAHN	FLOWERS AND COLORS
ZUJAJAT	زجاجة	ZOO-JAH-JAHT	GLASS CUP
ZUMURRUD	زورد	ZOO-MOO-ROOD	EMERALD

English-Arabic

And to create the Mare
God spoke to the South Wind.

"I will create from you a being which will be
a happiness to the good and
a misfortune to the bad.
Happiness shall be on its back,
and joy in the possessor."

–THE HOLY KORAN

Mouher (Colt)

ENGLISH	ARABIC		PRONUNCIATION
		– A –	
ABANDONED	MATROUK	حتروكه	MAH-TROOK
ABSTRACT, DRAWS ATTENTION AWAY FROM	MUJARRAD	مجرد	MOO-JAH-RAD
ABUNDANT	ZAYEED	زايد	ZAH-YEED
ACT OF TRAVELING ABOUT	JAWALAN	جوالان	JAH-WAH-LAHN
ACTOR	MOUMASSEL	موسل	MOO-MAH-SSEL
ADORNMENT	TAZWEEN	تزوينه	TAHZ-WEEN
ADVICE	NASSEEHA	نصيحة	NAH-SEE-HAH
ADVISOR, MINISTER	WAZEER	وزير	WAH-ZEER
ADVOCATE	MOUNADEL	مناضل	MOO-NAH-DEL
AFFECTIONATE, TENDER PASSION	HANOON	حنونه	HAH-NOON
AFFLUENT	JAZEEL	جزيل	JAH-ZEEL
AGITATOR	MOOHAREK	محركه	MOO-HAH-REK
ALERT, SMART	FAHEEM	فهيم	FAH-HEEM
ALMOND	LOWZ	لوز	LOWZ
ALONE	MUTAFARRED	متفرد	MOO-TAH-FAH-RED
AMATEUR	HAWEE	هاوي	HAH-WEE
AMBASSADOR	SAFEER	سفير	SAH-FEER
AN ENVOY	WAFD	وفد	WAHFD
ANCESTOR, GRANDFATHER	AJDAD	أجداد	AHJ-DAD
ANCIENT	KADEEM	قديم	KAH-DEEM
ANGEL	MALAK	ملاك	MAH-LAHK
ANGELIC	SAMAWEE	سماوي	SAH-MAH-WEE
ANIMATED, PLAYFUL	BASHOOSH	بشوش	BAH-SHOOSH
ANNOUNCER OF NEWS	MOUBASHER	مبشر	MOO-BAH-SHER

Mouhra (Filly)

ENGLISH	ARABIC		PRONUNCIATION
		– A –	
ABANDONED	MATROUKAH	مترركة	MAH-TROO-KAH
ABSTRACT, DRAWS ATTENTION AWAY FROM	MUJARADEH	مجردة	MOO-JAH-RAH-DEH
ABUNDANT	ZAYEEDAH	زييدة	ZAH-YEE-DAH
ACTIVE, ENERGETIC, EAGER	NASHEETAH	ناشيطة	NAH-SHEE-TAH
ACTOR	MOUMASSILAH	ممسلى	MOO-MAHS-SEE-LAH
ADORNMENT	TAZWEENAH	تزوينة	TAHZ-WEE-NAH
ADVICE, WORD TO THE WISE	NASEEHAH	نصيحة	NAH-SEE-HAH
ADVOCATE	MOUNADEELAH	مناضلة	MOO-NAH-DEE-LAH
AFFECTIONATE, TENDER PASSION	HANOONEH	حنونة	HAH-NOO-NEH
AFFLUENT	JAZEELAH	جزيلة	JAH-ZEE-LAH
AGENT, SUBSTITUTE	WAKILAT	وكيلة	WAH-KEE-LAHT
AGITATOR	MOOHAREEKAH	محركة	MOO-HAH-REE-KAH
ALONE	MOOTAFAREEDAH	منفردة	MOO-TAH-FAH-REE-DAH
AMATEUR	HAWEEYAH	حاوية	HAH-WEE-YAH
AMBASSADOR	SAFEERAH	سفيرة	SAH-FEE-RAH
AMBER	KAHRAMAN	قهرمانة	KAH-RAH-MAHN
ANARCHY	FAWDA	فوضة	FAHW-DAH
ANCIENT	KADIMAH	قديمة	KAH-DEE-MAH
ANGEL	MALAKEH	ملاكة	MAH-LAH-KEH
ANGELIC	SAMAWHIYAH	سماوية	SAH-MAH-WEE-YAH
ANIMATED, PLAYFUL	BASHOOSHAH	بشوشة	BAH-SHOO-SHAH
APPEARANCE	BOUROUZ	بروز	BOO-ROOZ
APPROACH, MOVE TOWARD	IKTERAB	إقتراب	IK-TEE-RAB
APRICOT	MESHMESHAH	مشمشة	MESH-MEH-SHAH

Mouher (Colt)

ENGLISH	ARABIC		PRONUNCIATION
– A –			
APPROACH	IKTIRAB	إشتراب	IK-TEE-RAB
ARENA, SQUARE	MEYDAN	حيبانه	MEH-DAHN
ASHES, COAL	JAMR	جمر	JAHMR
ASTRONOMER, FUTURE TELLER	FALAKEE	خلاتى	FAH-LAH-KEE
ASTUTE	SHATER	شاطر	SHAH-TEHR
AT ONCE	FAWRAN	فوراه	FAHW-RAN
AT YOUR ORDER OR SERVICE	AMRAK	أمرك	AHM-RAHK
ATTACK	HOUJOUM	هجوم	HOO-JOOM
ATTRACTIVE	JAZEB	جازب	JAH-ZEHB
AUTUMN	KHARIF	خريفه	KHAH-REEF
AWAKE	SAHRAN	سهراه	SAH-RAHN
– B –			
BAD BOY	SHARRIR	حشاريو	SHAH-REER
BADBOY (IN A PLAYFUL WAY)	RAZEEL	رزيل	RAH-ZEEL
BADGE OF HONOR	WEESAM	وديسام	WEE-SAHM
BALANCE OF ACCOUNT	RASID	رصيد	RAH-SEED
BARREL	BARMEEL	برميل	BAHR-MEEL
BASTARD	BANDOUK	بندوقه	BAN-DOOK
BATTALION	TABOUR	طبور	TAH-BOOR
BEARER OF GOOD NEWS	BASHAR	بشثار	BAH-SHAHR
BEARER OF GOOD NEWS	BASHIR	بشيس	BAH-SHEER
BEAUTIFUL	JAMIL	جميل	JAH-MEEL
BEAUTIFUL BOY, BEAUTIFUL SON	IBN JAMEEL	إبنه جميل	IBN-JAH-MEEL
BEAUTIFUL, OH BEAUTIFUL	JAMEEL YAH JAMEEL	جميل ياجميل	JAH-MEEL-YAH-JAH-MEEL

Mouhra (Filly)

ENGLISH	ARABIC		PRONUNCIATION

– A –

ENGLISH	ARABIC		PRONUNCIATION
ARSENAL	TERSANEH	ترسانة	TER-SAH-NEH
ASHES	REEMAD	ريماد	REE-MAD
ASSOCIATION	IRTIBAT	إرطباط	IR-TEE-BAHT
ASTUTE	SHATEERAH	شاطرة	SHAH-TEE-RAH
AT ONCE	FAURAN	فوراً	FAW-RAN
AT YOUR ORDER	AMREK	أمرك	AHM-REK
ATTACK, RUSH	HAJMEH	هجمة	HAHJ-MEH
ATTRACTIVE	JAZEEBAH	جاذبية	JAH-ZEE-BAH
AWAKE	SAHRANEH	سهرانة	SAH-RAH-NEH

– B –

ENGLISH	ARABIC		PRONUNCIATION
BAD GIRL (PLAYFUL WAY)	RAZEELAH	رزيلة	RAH-ZEE-LAH
BAY (COLOR)	HAMRAH	حمرا	HAM-RAH
BEAUTIFUL AND A BUNDLE OF ENERGY	NASHEETAH WE HELWAH	نشيطة	NAH-SHEE-TAH-WEH-HEL-WAH
BEAUTIFUL FILLY	MOUHRA HELWEH	مهرة حلوة	MOOH-RAH-HEL-WEH
BEAUTIFUL GIRL, BEAUTIFUL DAUGHTER	BINT HELWAH	بنت حلوة	BINT-HEL-WAH
BEAUTIFUL, GRACEFUL	JAMEELAH	جاميلة	JAH-MEE-LAH
BEAUTIFUL, VERY ATTRACTIVE	HELWAH	حلوة	HEL-WAH
BEAUTY	HASSANIEH	حسانية	HAHS-SAH-NEE-EH
BEAUTY, GODLINESS	MALAHAT	ملاحة	MAH-LAH-HAT
BEAUTY, GRACE	TALAWAT	طلاوة	TAH-LAH-WAHT
BEDOUIN, NOMAD	BADAWIEH	بداوية	BAH-DAH-WEE-YEH
BEE	NAHLAT	نحلات	NAH-LAHT
BENEDICTION	BARAKAT	بركات	BAH-RAH-KAHT
BIRD	ZAGLOULEH	زغلولة	ZAHG-LOO-LEH

129

Mouher (Colt)

ENGLISH	ARABIC		PRONUNCIATION
		– B –	
BEAUTY	GAMAL	جمال	GAH-MAHL
BEDOUIN, DESERT MAN	NOORI	نوري	NOO-REE
BEDOUIN, NOMAD	BADAWI	بداوي	BAH-DAH-WEE
BENEDICTION	BARAKAT	بركات	BAH-RAH-KAHT
BIRTH	MEELAHD	ميلاد	MEE-LAHD
BLACK	ASWAD	الاسود	AS-WAHD
BLACKSMITH	HADDAD	حداد	HAH-DAD
BLESSED	MARZOUK	مرزوقه	MAHR-ZOOK
BLESSED ONE	MOUBARAK	موباركه	MOO-BAH-RACK
BOLD, FORTHRIGHT	JASSEHR	جسار	JAH-SEHR
BOLDNESS, COURAGE	JASSARAT	جسارة	JAH-SAH-RAHT
BORN	MAULOOD	ولود	MAHW-LOOD
BORN	MAWLUUD	مولود	MAHW-LOOD
BRAINLESS, NO COMMON SENSE	MALTOUSH	ملطوش	MAL-TOOSH
BRAVE	SHAHJIH	شجيع	SHAH-JEE
BRAVEST OF THE BRAVE	KAHAR AL ABTAL	قهار الابطال	KAH-HAHR-AHL-AB-TAHL
BREEZE	NASIM	نسيم	NAH-SEEM
BRETHREN	IKHWAN	إخوانه	IKH-WAHN
BRIDEGROOM	ARISS	عريس	AH-REES
BRIDGE	JISR	جسر	JISER
BRIGHT	MUNIR	منير	MOO-NEER
BROCADE	DEEBAJ	ديباج	DEE-BAHJ
BROKER	DALLAL	دلّال	DAH-LAHL
BULKY	JASIM	جسيم	JAH-SEEM

Mouhra (Filly)

ENGLISH	ARABIC		PRONUNCIATION
		– B –	
BIRD OF PREY	KAWATHER	كواثر	KAH-WAH-THER
BIRTH	MEELADAH	ميلادة	MEE-LAH-DAH
BLACK ONE	SAWDAH	سعودة	SAHW-DAH
BLACKNESS	DOUHMAT	دهمة	DOOH-MAHT
BLAME, CENSURE	LOWM	لوم	LAUM
BLESSED	MARZOUKAH	مرزوقة	MAHR-ZOO-KAH
BLESSED ONE	MOUBARAKEH	مباركة	MOO-BAH-RAH-KEH
BLESSING	BARAKEH	بركة	BAH-RAH-KEH
BLUE COLOR	ZARKAH	زرقة	ZAR-KAH
BLUE-GRAY COLOR	ZARKAWI	زرقاوي	ZAR-KAH-WEE
BOLD AND BEAUTIFUL	JASSIRAH WAH HELWAH	جسيرة	JAH-SEE-RAH-WAH-HEL-WAH
BOLD AND STUBBORN	JAHSEERAH WAH ANIDAH	جسيرة	JAH-SEE-RAH-WAH-AH-NEE-DAH
BOLD, COURAGEOUS	JASOORAH	جسورة	JAH-SOO-RAH
BOLD, FORTHRIGHT	JASSIRAH	جاسيرة	JAH-SEE-RAH
BORN	MAULOODAH	مولودة	MAHW-LOO-DAH
BORN EARLY	MAWLUDAH BAKEER	مولودة بكير	MAHW-LOO-DAH-BAH-KEER
BRAINLESS, NO COMMON SENSE	MALTOUSHAH	ملطوشة	MAL-TOO-SHAH
BREATH OF LIFE	NASMAT	نسمة	NAHS-MAHT
BRIBE	RASHWAT	رشوة	RASH-WAHT
BRIDE	AROUSSAH	عروسة	AH-ROOS-SAH
BRIGHT	MOONIRAH	منيرة	MOO-NEE-RAH
BRINGS GOOD NEWS	BASHARAH	بشارة	BAH-SHAH-RAH
BROKER	DALLALLEH	دلالة	DAH-LAH-LEH
BROWNISH COLOR	SAMRAH	سمرة	SAHM-RAH

131

Mouher (Colt)

ENGLISH	ARABIC		PRONUNCIATION
	– B –		
BULLY, EXCESSIVE	FAHESH	فاحش	FAH-HESH
BURGLAR, THIEF	HARAMI	حرامي	HAH-RAH-MEE
BUTCHER	JAZZAR	جزار	JAH-ZAHR
BUTTERFLY (LIGHT, FLOATY)	FARASHEH	فراشة	FAH-RAH-SHEH
	– C –		
CAMEL	JAMAL	جمال	JAH-MAHL
CAMPHOR	KAFOUR	كافور	KAH-FOOR
CANARY	BOOLBOOL	بلبل	BOOL-BOOL
CASTLE	KASR	قصر	KAHSER
CAVALRY	KHAYALEEN	خيالين	KHAH-YAH-LEEN
CELEBRITY	ISHTIHAR	إشتهار	ISH-TEE-HAR
CHARM, SPELL, BEWITCH	JAHZAHBAT	جزابة	JAH-ZAH-BAHT
CHATTING, TALKING	DARDASHAH	دردشة	DAHR-DAH-SHAH
CHERRY, CHERRY TREE	KARAZ	كرز	KAH-RAHZ
CHESTNUT	ASHQUAR	أشقر	AHSH-KAR
CHIEF	WALI	والي	WAH-LEE
CHIEF OF THE HOUSE	WALI AL BEIT	والي البيت	WAH-LEE-AHL-BEIT
CHIEF, PRINCE	WAJEEH	وجيه	WHAH-JEEH
CLANDESTINE	MAKTOUM	مكتوم	MAHK-TOOM
CLEAR	SAFI	صافي	SAH-FEE
CLEAR COOL PURE WATER	ZOULAL	زولال	ZOO-LAHL
CLEAR, DISTINCT	ZAHIR	ظاهر	ZAH-HER
CLIMB	SAUD	صعود	SAH-OOD
CLOGS	KIBKAB	كبكاب	KEEB-KAHB

Mouhra (Filly)

ENGLISH	ARABIC		PRONUNCIATION
		– B –	
BULKY, OVERSIZED	JAHSEEMAH	جاسيمة	JAH-SEE-MAH
BUSY	MASHGOOLEH	مشغولة	MAHSH-GOO-LEH
BUTTERFLY (FLOATY AND LIGHT)	FARASHAH	فراشة	FAH-RAH-SHAH
BUTTERFLY (FLOATY AND LIGHT)	FARASHEH	فراشة	FAH-RAH-SHEH
		– C –	
CALAMITY, TROUBLE	DAHIYAT	دهية	DAH-HEE-YAHT
CALM, SETTLED	RAKEEZEH	رأيزة	RAH-KEE-ZEH
CANARY	BULBULAH	بولبلة	BOOL-BOO-LAH
CANDLE	SHAMAH	شمعة	SHAHM-AH
CERTAIN, FOR SURE	AKEEDAH	أكيدة	AH-KEE-DAH
CERTAINTY, WITHOUT A DOUBT	DAHIAT	داهية	DAH-HEE-YAHT
CHANCE	SADFAT	صدفات	SAHD-FAHT
CHARM, SPELL, BEWITCH	JAHZAHBAT	جرابة	JAH-ZAH-BAHT
CHATTING, TALKING	DARDASHA	دردشة	DAHR-DAH-SHAH
CHEEK, FACE	WAJNAT	وجنات	WAHJ-NAHT
CHEERFUL OR GENTLE FACE	BASHASHAH	بشاشة	BAH-SHAH-SHAH
CHERISHED OBJECT, GIFT	TEHFAT	تحفات	TEH-FAHT
CHERRY, BEAD	KARAZEH	كرزة	KAH-RAH-ZEH
CHIEF	WALIYAH	ولية	WAH-LEE-YAH
CLANDESTINE	MAKTOUMAH	مكتومة	MAHK-TOO-MAH
CLEVER, CUNNING	ZAKIYAH	زكية	ZAH-KEE-YAH
CLOSE FRIEND	NADEEMAH	نديمة	NAH-DEE-MAH
CLOSENESS TO, SPECIAL BOND	AZIZAH	عزيزة	AH-ZEE-ZAH
CLUMSY	RASHEEMAH	رشيمة	RAH-SHEE-MAH

Mouher (Colt)

ENGLISH	ARABIC		PRONUNCIATION
		– C –	
CLOSE FRIEND	NADEEM	نديم	NAH-DEEM
CLOSENESS TO SOMEONE	AZIZ	عزيز	AH-ZEEZ
CLUMSY	RASHEEM	رشيم	RAH-SHEEM
COLD	BARD	برد	BARD
COLOR	LOWN	لونه	LOUN
COLORFUL	MOULAWAN	مولونه	MOO-LAH-WAHN
COLORS	ALWAN	علوانه	AHL-WAHN
COLT	MOUHER	موحر	MOO-HER
COMBAT, STRUGGLE	JEHAD	جهاد	JEE-HAD
COMMISSARY	WAKIL	وكيل	WAH-KEEL
COMPANION	RAFIK	رفيقه	RAH-FEEK
COMPASSIONATE	RAHEEM	رحيم	RAH-HEEM
COMPLETE	TAMAM	تمام	TAH-MAM
COMRADE	ZAMIL	زميل	ZAH-MEEL
CONCEITED	FASSHEET	فشيط	FAH-SHEET
CONCEITED, SELF ASSURED	ISTIKBAR	إستكبار	ISS-TIK-BAR
CONCEITED, SELF ASSURED	MOUTAKABER	متكبد	MOO-TAH-KAH-BER
CONQUERER	NASSER	ناصر	NAH-SER
CONQUERER OF THE FAITH	NASSER AL DEEN	نصر الدين	NAH-SER-AHL-DEEN
CONQUEROR	FATEH	فاتح	FAH-TEH
CONQUEROR	KAHAR	قههار	KAH-HAHR
CONTINUOUS, EVERLASTING	DAHYEM	دايم	DAH-YEHM
CONVICTION	YAKEEN	ياكين	YAH-KEEN
CORAL	MERJAN	مرجانه	MEHR-JAHN

Mouhra (Filly)

ENGLISH	ARABIC		PRONUNCIATION
		– C –	
COLORATION FLEA BITTEN GREY	DIBBANI	دباني	DEEB-BAH-NEE
COLORS	ALWAN	ألوان	AHL-WAHN
COMMANDER	HAKIMAH	حاكمة	HAH-KEE-MAH
COMMISSARIES	WAKEELAT	وكيلات	WAH-KEE-LAHT
COMPANION	RAFEEKAH	رفيقة	RAH-FEE-KAH
COMPANION, FRIEND	ZAMILEH	زميلة	ZAH-MEE-LEH
COMPANY	RIFKAT	رفقة	REEF-KAHT
COMPASSION	RAHMAT	رحمة	RAH-MAHT
COMPASSION FOR YOU	RAHMAT ALEKEE	رحمة عليك	RAH-MAHT-AH-LEH-KEE
COMPASSIONATE	RAHEEMEH	رحيمة	RAH-HEE-MEH
COMPLETE	KAHMILAH	كاملة	KAH-MEE-LAH
CONCEITED	FASHEETAH	نشيطة	FAH-SHEE-TAH
CONCEITED, SELF ASSURED	ISTIKBAR	إستكبار	ISS-TIK-BAR
CONCEITED, SELF ASSURED	MOUTAKABERAH	متكبرة	MOO-TAH-KAH-BEH-RAH
CONFUSION	DAHSHAT	دهشة	DAH-SHAHT
CONQUEROR	NASIRAH	ناصرة	NAH-SEE-RAH
CONSIDERATION, POSITION	WAJAHAT	وجاهة	WAH-JAH-HAHT
CONSOLATION	SULWAN	سلوان	SOOL-WAHN
CONTINUOUS	DAYEEMAH	دايمة	DAH-YEE-MAH
CORAL	MERJANEH	مرجانة	MEHR-JAH-NEH
COUNTRIES UNITED	EMARAT	إمارات	EE-MAH-RAHT
COURAGE	JASSARA	جسارة	JAH-SAH-RAH
CROWD, REPUBLIC	JAHMHOURIEH	جمهورية	JAHM-HOO-RIEH
CROWNED	MOUTAWAJEH	متوجة	MOU-TAH-WAH-JEH

135

Mouher (Colt)

ENGLISH	ARABIC		PRONUNCIATION
		– C –	
COUNTRY	WATAN	وطنه	WAH-TAN
COURAGEOUS	JASSUR	جسور	JAH-SOOR
CREED, BELIEF	EMAN	إيمانه	EE-MAHN
CROCIDILE	TEMSAH	تمساح	TEM-SAH
CROWD	JAHMHOUR	جمهور	JAHM-HOOR
CROWNED	MOUTAWAJ	موتوج	MOU-TAH-WAHJ
CRYSTALLITE	ZABARDAJ	زبردج	ZAH-BAR-DAJ
CUP	FENJAHN	فنجانه	FEN-JAHN
CURIOUS, INQUISITIVE	HAIRAN	حيرانه	HAI-RAHN
CUTE	KARBOUJ	كربوج	KAHR-BOOJ
		– D –	
DAMASCUS (SYRIA'S CAPITAL)	AL SHAM	الشام	AHL-SHAM
DANCER	RAGUASS	رقاص	RAH-GUASS
DANCER	RAKKAS	رقاص	RAH-KAS
DANGEROUS	KATIR	خطير	KHAH-TEER
DARK	DAMIS	دامس	DAH-MEES
DARK COMPLEXION	ASMAR	أسمر	AHS-MAR
DARK OF COLOR	RAMIK	رامك	RAH-MEEK
DAVID	DAOUD	داود	DAH-OOD
DAWN, DAYBREAK	FAJR	فجر	FAJR
DAY	NAHAR	نهار	NAH-HAHR
DEACON	SHAMAS	شماس	SHAH-MAS
DEAR TO SOMEONE	AZEEZ	عزيز	AH-ZEEZ
DECEIVER	DAJJAL	دجال	DAH-JAHL

Mouhra (Filly)

ENGLISH	ARABIC		PRONUNCIATION
		– C –	
CURIOUS, INQUISITIVE	HAIRANEH	حيرانة	HAI-RAH-NEH
CUTE AND SASSY	GHANOUJEH	غنوجة	GHAH-NOO-JEH
CUTE AS THE MOON	AMURRAH	أمورة	AH-MOUR-RAH
CUTE, ATTRACTIVE	KARBOUJEH	كربوجة	KAHR-BOO-JEH
		– D –	
DAMASCUS	DIMASHK	دمشق	DEE-MASHK
DAMSEL, YOUNG GIRL	JAHRIAT	جارية	JAH-REE-YAHT
DANCER	RAQUASSAH	رقاصة	RAH-KAH-SAH
DANGEROUS	KHATIRAH	خطيرة	KHAH-TEE-RAH
DARK AND PRETTY	SAMRAH WI HELWEH	سمرة وحلوة	SAHM-RAH-WEH-HELWEH
DARLING, DEAR TO SOMEONE	AZEEZAH	عزيزة	AH-ZEE-ZAH
DAUGHTER OF THE NILE	BINT EL NIL	بنت النيل	BINT-EL-NEEL
DAUGHTER OF THE PEACE	BINT EL SALAM	بنت السلام	BINT-EL-SAH-LAHM
DAUGHTER OF THE WIND	BINT AL RIYAH	بنت الرياح	BINT-AHL-REE-YAH
DEAF ONE	TARSHAH	طرشة	TAR-SHAH
DEAR, MY BELOVED	HABIBTEE	حبيبتي	HAH-BEEB-TEE
DECADE, TIME PASSED	DUHUUR	دهور	DOO-HOOR
DECEIVER	DAJJALEH	دجالة	DAH-JAH-LEH
DECENT	LAYEEQAH	لايقة	LAH-YEE-KAH
DECORATION	ZINAHT	زينة	ZEE-NAHT
DEER, ANTELOPE	GHAZALEH	غزالة	GHA-ZAH-LEH
DEFEAT	INHEEZAM	انهزام	IN-HEE-ZAHM
DEFENDER	MOUDAFEAH	مدافعة	MOO-DAH-FEH-AH
DELICATE	NAZEEKAH	نزيقة	NAH-ZEE-KAH

Mouher (Colt)

ENGLISH	ARABIC		PRONUNCIATION
		– D –	
DECENT	LAYEQ	لايقة	LAH-YEK
DEER, ANTELOPE	GHAZAL	غزال	GHA-ZAHL
DEFEAT	INHEEZAM	إنهزام	IN-HEE-ZAM
DEFENDER	MOUDAFEH	مودافع	MOO-DAH-FEH
DEFIANCE	MOOARADAT	موواردات	MOO-AHR-AH-DAHT
DELICATE	NAZIK	نزيقة	NAH-ZEEK
DELIGHTFUL	LAZEEZ	لزيز	LAH-ZEEZ
DEPUTY	NAYEB	نايب	NAH-YEB
DERVISH, SIMPLE	DARWISH	درويش	DAHR-WEESH
DESPAIR	EYAS	إياس	EE-YAHS
DESTINY, FATE	NASEEB	نصيب	NAH-SEEB
DESTRUCTIVE ONE	DAMMAR	دمار	DAHM-MAHR
DEVIL	EBLIS	إبليس	EB-LYSS
DEVOTED	MOUKLIS	مخلص	MOOK-LEESS
DICTATOR	ZALEM	ظالم	ZAH-LEM
DIFFICULT	KASSEE	خاسي	KAH-SEE
DILIGENCE	IJTEHAD	إجتهاد	IJ-TEE-HAD
DIRECTION FOR ALLAH	ILHAM	إلهام	EEL-HAM
DIVINE	RABBANI	رباني	RAH-BAH-NEE
DOMINANT ONE	MOUSAYTAR	موحيطر	MOO-SIGH-TAHR
DOORMAN	BAWAHB	بواب	BAH-WAHB
DOVE	HAMAM	حمام	HAH-MAHM
DREAMS	AHLAM	احلام	AH-LAHM
DRESSED	LABESS	لابس	LAH-BESS

Mouhra (Filly)

ENGLISH	ARABIC		PRONUNCIATION

– D –

ENGLISH	ARABIC	PRONUNCIATION
DELIGHTFUL	LAZEEZAH	لزيزة	LAH-ZEE-ZAH
DEPUTY	NAYEEBAH	نايبة	NAH-YEE-BAH
DERVISH, SIMPLE	DARWISHAH	دوريشة	DAR-WEE-SHAH
DESERT	BADIEH	بادية	BAH-DEE-YEH
DESERT	BARRIEH	برية	BAHR-REE-YEH
DESERT	SAHRA	صحرة	SAH-RAH
DESERT PERSON	NOORIYAH	نورية	NOO-REE-YAH
DESIRE	TALBAT	طلبت	TAL-BAHT
DESTRUCTIVE ONE	DAMMARAH	دماره	DAHM-MAH-RAH
DEVILISHNESS	SHAYTANAT	شيطانة	SHAHY-TAH-NAHT
DEVOTED	MUKLEESSAH	ملصة	MOO-KLEE-SSAH
DIAMOND	ALMASE	ألماسة	AHL-MAH-SEH
DICTATOR	ZAIMAH	زاعيمة	ZAH-EE-MAH
DIFFERENT, UNUSUAL	SHAWARED	شوارد	SHAH-WAH-RED
DIFFICULT	KASSEEYAH	قاسية	KAH-SEE-YAH
DIGNITY, GRAVITY	RAZANAT	رزانات	RAH-ZAH-NAHT
DILIGENCE	IJTEHAD	إجتهاد	IJ-TEE-HAD
DIRECTION FOR ALLAH	ILHAM	إلهام	EEL-HAM
DISHONEST, LIAR	KAHZABEH	كزابة	KAH-ZAH-BEH
DIVERSION	SALWAT	سلوة	SAHL-WAHT
DIVINE	RABBANIAH	ربانية	RAH-BAH-NEE-YAH
DOMESTIC	AHLIEH	أهلية	AHL-LEE-YEH
DOORWOMAN	BAWAHBAH	بوابة	BAH-WAH-BAH
DOVE	HAMAMEE	حمامة	HAH-MAH-MEE

Mouher (Colt)

ENGLISH	ARABIC		PRONUNCIATION
		– D –	
DRINKS	SHARAB	شراب	SHAH-RAHB
DRUM PRAYER	TABBAL	طبال	TAH-BAL
DRY ONE	YABESS	يابس	YAH-BESS
DUTY	LAWAZEM	لوازم	LAH-WAH-ZEM
DUTY	WAJEB	واجب	WHAH-JEB
		– E –	
EAGER, FULL OF ENERGY	NASHEET	ناشيط	NAH-SHEET
EAGLE	NISR	نسر	NEESR
EAGLE	SAKR	صقر	SAHKR
EARLY	BAKKIR	بكير	BAHK-KEER
EARNEST	IHTEMAM	احتمام	IH-TEE-MAM
EARTHQUAKE	ZILZAL	زلزال	ZIL-ZAHL
ECHO	SADA	صدا	SAH-DAH
ECLIPSE	INKISAF	إنكساف	IN-KEE-SAHF
EGOTISTIC	ANANIYAT	أنانيات	AH-NAH-NEE-YAHT
EGYPT	MASR	مصر	MAHSER
EGYPTIAN	MASRI	مصري	MAHS-REE
EIGHTH LUNAR MONTH	SHAABAN	شعبانه	SHAH-BAN
ELEGANT	AZRAFF	أزرفه	AZ-RAHF
ELEVATED ONE	ALI	على	AH-LEE
EMPTY	AL-KHALI	الخالي	AHL-KAH-LEE
ENTIRE, COMPLETE	KAMEL	كامل	KAH-MEL
EQUILIBRIUM	ETTIZAN	إتزانه	IT-TEEZ-AHN
ESCAPEE	HAZEEM	حازيم	HAH-ZEEM

140

Mouhra (Filly)

ENGLISH	ARABIC		PRONUNCIATION
		– D –	
DOVE	YAMAMAT	ياماية	YAH-MAH-MAHT
DREAMS	AHLAM	احلام	AH-LAHM
DRESSED	LABEESSAH	لابسة	LAH-BEE-SAH
DRINKS	SHARAB	شراب	SHAH-RAHB
DRUM PRAYER	TABBALEH	طبالة	TAH-BAH-LEH
DRY ONE	YABISSAH	يابسة	YAH-BEE-SAH
DUTY	LAWAZEM	لوازم	LAH-WAH-ZEM
		– E –	
EARNEST	IHTEMAM	إحتمام	IH-TEE-MAM
EARTHQUAKE	ZILZALEH	زلزاله	ZIL-ZAH-LEH
EAST	SHARQ	شرق	SHARK
ECHO	SADAH	صدا	SAH-DAH
ECLIPSE	INKISAF	إنخساف	IN-KEE-SAHF
ECLIPSE	KOUSOUF	كسوفه	KOO-SOOF
EGOTISTIC	ANANIYAT	أنانيت	AH-NAH-NEE-YAHT
ELEGANT	ZARIFFAH	ظريفة	ZAH-REE-FAH
ELEGANT FORM, SLENDER	RASHEIKAH	رشيقة	RAH-SHEE-KAH
ELEVATED ONE	ALIAH	علية	AH-LEE-YAH
EMERALD	ZUMURRUD	زمورد	ZOO-MOO-ROOD
ENCLOSURE	HAZIRAH	حازيرة	HAH-ZEE-RAH
END, UTMOST POINT	NIHAYAT	نيهاية	NEE-HAH-YAHT
EQUILIBRIUM	TAWAZUN	توازن	TAH-WAH-ZOON
ESCAPEE	HAZEEMAH	هزيمة	HAH-ZEE-MAH
ETERNAL	AZALEH	أزاله	AH-ZAH-LEH

Mouher (Colt)

ENGLISH	ARABIC	PRONUNCIATION
– E –		
ETERNAL, FOREVER, ENDLESS	EILA AL ABAD	إلا الابد	EELAH-AL-AH-BAHD
EUROPEAN MAN	EFRANJE	إفرنجي	IF-FRAN-JEE
EVERGREEN	SINDIYAN	سنديانة	SIN-DEE-YAN
EVIDENT	ZAHER	ظاهر	ZAH-HER
EVIL, SATAN	SHEETAN	شيطانة	SHEE-TAN
EVOLUTION	TAHLEEL	تحليل	TAH-LEEL
EXCELLENT	JAYED	جايد	JAH-YED
EXCEPTIONAL	FARID	فريد	FAH-REED
EXCESS FAVOR, EXCELLENCE	FADL	فضل	FAHDL
EXCITED, EXUBERANT	HAYJAN	هيجانة	HAY-JAHN
EXCITED, UPSET, UNSETTTLED	BITRAN	بطرانة	BIT-RAHN
EXCITEMENT	HIYAHJ	هياج	HEE-YAHJ
EXECUTIONER	JALLAD	جلاد	JAH-LLAHD
EXISTENCE, NATURE	KIYAN	كيانة	KEE-YAHN
EXPERIMENT	EKTIBAR	إختبار	ICK-TEE-BAHR
EXPLOSION	INFIJAR	إنفجار	IN-FEE-JAHR
EXTERMINATOR	DAHMAR	دحار	DAH-MAHR
– F –		
FAILURE	FASHAL	فشل	FAH-SHALL
FAITHFUL TO HIS COUNTRY	WATANI	وطني	WAH-TAH-NEE
FAME OF THE ORIGIN	SHUHRAT AL NASSAB	شهرة	SHOOH-RAHT-AHL-NAH-SAB
FAREWELL	WEEDAA	وداع	WEE-DAA
FARMER, COUNTRYMAN	FALLAH	فلاح	FAH-LAH
FAT	DASSIM	دسيم	DAH-SEEM

Mouhra (Filly)

ENGLISH	ARABIC		PRONUNCIATION
		– E –	
EUROPEAN WOMAN	EFRANJIYEH	إفرنجية	IF-FRAN-JEE-YEH
EVENING	LEYLEH	ليلة	LEH-LEH
EVERLASTING	DAHYEEMAH	دائمة	DAH-YEE-MAH
EVIL, SATAN	SHEETANEH	شيطانة	SHEE-TAN-NEH
EXCELLENT	JAYEDAH	جيدة	JAH-YEH-DAH
EXCEPTIONAL	FARIDAH	فريدة	FAH-REE-DAH
EXCESSIVE LOVE	SABABA	صبابة	SAH-BAH-BAH
EXCITED, EXUBERANT	HAYJANNEH	هيجانة	HAY-JAH-NEH
EXCITED, UPSET, UNSETTLED	BITRAHNEH	مطرانة	BIT-RAH-NEH
EXCITEMENT	HIYAHJ	هياج	HEE-YAHJ
EXCUSE, PRETEXT	HUJJAT	حجة	HUHJ-JAHT
EXECUTIONER	JALLADEH	جلادة	JAH-LAH-DEH
		– F –	
FAITHFUL TO ONE'S COUNTRY	WATANIAH	وطنية	WAH-TAH-NEE-YAH
FAME	SHOUHRAH	شهرة	SHOUH-RAH
FAMOUS	SHAHEERAH	شاهيرة	SHAH-HEE-RAH
FARMER, COUNTRY WOMAN	FALLAHAH	فلاحة	FAH-LAH-HAH
FASHION STYLE, MODE	KASM	كسم	KAHSM
FAT	DASSIMEH	داسيمة	DAH-SEE-MEH
FATE	NAHSIBAH	نسيبة	NAH-SEE-BAH
FEAR	RAHBAT	رهبة	RAH-BAHT
FEARFUL, SCARY	RAHEEBAH	راهيبة	RAH-HEE-BAH
FEMALE MILITARY MEMBER	JUNDIYAH	جندية	JUN-DEE-YAH
FEMALE SOLDIER	JUNDIYEH	جندية	JUN-DEE-YEH

Mouher (Colt)

ENGLISH	ARABIC		PRONUNCIATION
		– F –	
FEARFUL, SCARY	RAHEEB	رهيب	RAH-HEEB
FINE BODY	RASHEIK AL JISM	رشيق الجسم	RAH-SHEEK-AHL-JISM
FIRE	HARIK	حريقة	HAH-REEK
FIRM, PAVED ROAD	RASIF	رصيفة	RAH-SEEF
FIRST	AWWAL	أول	AHW-WAHL
FIRST BORN	BIKR	بكر	BEEKR
FIVE	KHAMSA	خمسة	KAHM-SAH
FLAME, BLAZE	LAHEEB	لاهيب	LAH-HEEB
FLASH, BRIGHTNESS	LAMAAN	لمعانة	LAH-MAHN
FLIGHT, ESCAPE	FERAR	فرار	FEE-RAHR
FLOOD, DELUGE	TAWAFAN	طوفانة	TAH-WAH-FAHN
FLOWERS	ZUHUR	زهور	ZOO-HOOR
FLUENT IN LANGUAGE	FASEEH	فصيح	FAH-SEAH
FOLLOWER	LAHIQ	لاحقة	LAH-HIQ
FOLLOWER OF THE RIGHT WAY	RASHID	رشيد	RAH-SHEED
FOOD	FALAFEL	فلافل	FAH-LAH-FEL
FOR SURE, CERTAIN	AKEED	أكيد	AH-KEED
FORBIDDEN	HARAM	حرام	HAH-RAHM
FOREVER	ALATOUL	على طول	AHL-LA-TOOL
FORGIVEN ONE	MAGFOUR	مغفور	MAHG-FOOR
FORGIVING	GHAFER	غافر	GAH-FER
FORTUNE TELLER	BASSAR	بصار	BAH-SAHR
FOUNDATION	BUNIAT	بنية	BOO-NEE-AHT
FOUNTAINS	NAWAFIR	نوافير	NAH-WAH-FEER

Mouhra (Filly)

ENGLISH	ARABIC		PRONUNCIATION
		– F –	
FILLY	MOUHRA	مهرة	MOOH-RAH
FIRM, CERTAIN	AKIDEH	أكيدة	AH-KEE-DEH
FIRST	AWWALEH	أولة	AHW-WAH-LEH
FIRST BORN	BIKRAH	بكرة	BEEK-RAH
FIVE	KHAMSA	خمسة	KAHM-SAH
FLAGS	RAYAT	رايات	RAH-YAHT
FLAME	LAHBAT	لهبت	LAH-BAHT
FLOOD, DELUGE	TAWAFAN	طوفان	TAH-WAH-FAHN
FLOWER	ZAHRAH	زهرة	ZAH-RAH
FLOWERS	ZUHUR	زهور	ZOO-HOOR
FLOWERS AND COLORS	ZUHUR WA ALWAN	زهور والوان	ZOO-HOOR-WAH-AHL-WAHN
FLUENT IN LANGUAGE	FASEEHAH	فصيحة	FAH-SEE-HAH
FLUTE	RABABA	ربابة	RAH-BAH-BAH
FOLLOWER	LAHIQUAH	لاحقة	LAH-HEE-QUAH
FOR YOU ONLY	KIRMALEK	كرمالك	KEER-MAH-LEHK
FORBIDDEN	HARAM	حرام	HAH-RAHM
FOREHEAD	JABHA	جبهة	JAHB-HAH
FOREHEAD	JIBBAH	جباه	JIB-BAH
FORELOCK	NASSIAT	ناصية	NAHS-SEE-YAHT
FOREVER	KAHLIDAH	خالدة	KAH-LEE-DAH
FOREVER, IMMORTAL	DAYIMAH	دائمة	DAH-YEE-MAH
FORGIVEN ONE	MAGFOURAH	مغفورة	MAHG-FOO-RAH
FORTELLER OF THE FUTURE	MOUNJER	منجر	MOON-JER
FORTUNE TELLER	BASSARAH	بصارة	BAH-SAH-RAH

145

Mouher (Colt)

ENGLISH	ARABIC		PRONUNCIATION
		– F –	
FRAGILE, LEAN	NAHEEF	لخيفا	NAH-HEEF
FREE	BALASH	بلاش	BAH-LAHSH
FREEDOM	HOURRIAT	حرية	HOO-REE-YAHT
FRIEND	ZAMEEL	زاميل	ZAH-MEEL
FRIEND (of the road), TRAVELING COMPANION	RAFEEQ	رفيقه	RAH-FEEK
FRIEND FOR LIFE	ZAMEEL AL OUMR	زاميل العمر	ZAH-MEEL-AHL-OUMR
FROM DAMASCUS	SHAMEE	شامي	SHAH-MEE
FROM HELL	JAHANAMEE	جهنامي	JAH-HAH-NAH-MEE
FROM THE COUNTRY	BALADEE	بلدي	BAH-LAH-DEE
FROM THE COUNTRY	BALADI	بلدي	BAH-LAH-DEE
FROM THE HEART	NAFSANI	نفساني	NAF-SAH-NEE
FROM THE NORTH	SHAMALEE	شمالي	SHAH-MAH-LEE
FROM TOUNIS (in Middle East)	TOUNISEE	تونيسي	TOO-NEE-SEE
FULL MOON	BADR	بدر	BAHDER
FUNDAMENTAL	ASLEE	اصلي	AHS-LEE
FUTURE	MOUSTAKBEL	مستقبل	MOOS-TAHK-BELL
		– GG –	
GARDENER	BOUSTANI	بستاني	BOOS-TAH-NEE
GAURDSMAN	SHORTI	شرطي	SHOR-TEE
GELDING	TAWASH	طواش	TAH-WASH
GEM, PRECIOUS STONE	JAHWHAR	جوهر	JAHW-HAR
GENTLE, KIND	LATIF	لطيف	LAH-TEEF
GENUINE, TRUE, VIRTUOUS	SALEH	صالح	SAH-LEH
GIANT	GHOUL	غول	GOOL

Mouhra (Filly)

ENGLISH	ARABIC		PRONUNCIATION

– F –

ENGLISH	ARABIC		PRONUNCIATION
FOUNTAIN	FAWARAH	خوّارة	FAH-WAH-RAH
FOUNTAINS	NAWAFEER	نوافير	NAH-WAH-FEER
FRAGILE, LEAN	NAHEEFAH	نحيفة	NAH-HEE-FAH
FREE	BALASH	بلاش	BAH-LASH
FRESH BREATH	NAKHAT	نكهة	NAHK-HAHT
FRIEND (of the road), TRAVELING COMPANION	RAFIKAH	رفيقة	RAH-FEE-KAH
FRIENDSHIP	ELFAT	إلفة	EL-FAHT
FRINGE	SHARSHARAT	شرشرة	SHAHR-SHAH-RAHT
FROM DAMASCUS	SHAMIEH	شامية	SHAH-MEE-YEH
FROM HELL	JAHANAMIYAH	جهنّامية	JAH-HAH-NAH-MEE-YAH
FROM THE COUNTRY	BALADIEH	بلدية	BAH-LAH-DEE-YEH
FROM THE HEART	NAFSANIYAH	نفسانية	NAF-SAH-NEE-YAH
FROM THE NORTH	SHAMALIYAH	شمالية	SHAH-MAH-LEE-YAH
FROM TOUNIS (in Middle East)	TOUNISSIYAH	تونسية	TOO-NEE-SEE-YAH
FUNDAMENTALIST	ASLEEYAH	اصلية	AHS-LEE-YAH
FUR CLOAK	FARWAT	فروة	FAHR-WAHT

– G –

ENGLISH	ARABIC		PRONUNCIATION
GATHERING	BARKEH	بركة	BAR-KEH
GEM	JAWHARAH	جوهرة	JAHW-HAH-RAH
GENERAL HAPPINESS	FARAH	فرح	FAH-RAH
GENTLENESS	DAMAZAT	دمازات	DAH-MAH-ZAHT
GENUINE, SOUND, VIRTUOUS	SALEEHAH	صالحة	SAH-LEE-HAH
GIFT	HADIYAH	هدية	HAH-DEE-YAH
GIFT OF THE EYES	HADIYAT AL OYOUN	هدية العيون	HAH-DEE-YAHT-AHL-OU-YOON

Mouher (Colt)

ENGLISH	ARABIC		PRONUNCIATION
		– G –	
GIFT	HADIYA	صديه	HAH-DEE-YAH
GIFTS	HADIYAT	صديه	HAH-DEE-YAHT
GIVER, KIND, NOBLE	KARIM	كريم	KAH-REEM
GLANCE, A QUICK LOOK	NAZRAT	نظرة	NAHZ-RAHT
GLASS	ZEJAJ	زجاج	ZEE-JAJ
GLEAMING, SHINING	LAMEH	لامع	LAH-MEH
GOD'S SERVANT	ABDALLAH	عبدلله	AHB-DAH-LAH
GOING OUT	KHAREEJ	خارج	KAH-REEJ
GOLD COIN	DINAR	دينار	DEE-NAHR
GOOD	TAYEB	طيب	TAH-YEB
GOSSIP	DARDAHSHE	دردشة	DAHR-DAH-SHEH
GOVERNOR, COMMANDER	HAKEM	حاكم	HAH-KEM
GRACIOUSNESS	KARAMAH	كرامة	KAH-RAH-MAH
GRAMMATICAL	NAHAWEE	نحوي	NAH-HAH-WEE
GRAND, GREAT	KABEER	كبير	KAH-BEER
GRAND, MIGHTY	JALIL	جليل	JAH-LEEL
GRANDSON OF	HAFEED	حفيد	HAH-FEED
GRATEFUL	FADOOLEE	فاضولة	FAH-DOO-LEE
GRATEFUL	SHAHKER	شاكر	SHAH-KEHR
GREAT	JALEEL	جليل	JAH-LEEL
GREETINGS	SALAMAT	سلامة	SAH-LAH-MAHT
GRIEVED	LAHFAN	لهفانة	LAH-FAHN
GUARD, GROUNDS KEEPER	NATOUR	ناطور	NAH-TOOR
GUEST	NAZEEL	نزيل	NAH-ZEEL

Mouhra (Filly)

ENGLISH	ARABIC		PRONUNCIATION
		– G –	
GIFT OF THE SPIRIT	HADIYAT AL NOUFOUS	حديه النفوس	HAH-DEE-YAHT-AHL-NOO-FOOS
GIFT, BENEFIT	JADWAH	جدوة	JAHD-WAH
GIFT, FAVOR	MINHAT	منحة	MIN-HAHT
GIFTS	HADAYAH	هدايا	HAH-DAH-YAH
GIRAFFE	ZARAFAT	زرافة	ZAH-RAH-FAHT
GIRL FROM EGYPT	MASRIYAH	مصرية	MAHS-REE-YAH
GIVER, KIND	KAREEMAH	كريمة	KAH-REE-MAH
GLANCE, EYE-CATCHING	NAZRAT	نظرة	NAHZ-RAHT
GLANCE, EYE-CATCHING	LAMHAT	لمحة	LAHM-HAHT
GLASS CUP	ZUJAJAT	زجاجة	ZOO-JAH-JAHT
GOING OUT	KHAREEJAH	خارجة	KAH-REE-JAH
GOLDEN	ZAHABIEH	ذهبية	ZAH-HAH-BEE-YEH
GOOD	TAYEEBAH	طيبة	TAH-YEE-BAH
GOOD ANNOUNCEMENT	BOUSHRAH	بشرة	BOOSH-RAH
GOOD HEARTED	TAYYEBAH	طيبة	TAH-YEH-BAH
GOOD LIVING	RAFAHAT	رفاهة	RAH-FAH-HAHT
GOOD NEWS	TABASHIR	تباشير	TAH-BAH-SHEER
GOOD SEED	HASSENAT	حسنة	HAH-SSEH-NAHT
GOODNESS, EXCELLENCE	JAWDAT	جودة	JAHW-DAHT
GRACEFUL DANCER	RAKASSAH ANIKAH	رقاصة انيقة	RAH-KAHS-SAH-AH-NEE-KAH
GRACEFUL, KIND	LATIFAH	لطيفة	LAH-TEE-FAH
GRACIOUSNESS	KARAHMAH	كرامة	KAH-RAH-MAH
GRAIN, SEED	BIZREH	بزرة	BIZ-REH
GRAND	KABEERAH	كبيرة	KAH-BEE-RAH

Mouher (Colt)

ENGLISH	ARABIC		PRONUNCIATION
		– G –	
GUEST	ZAIR	زائر	ZAH-YEAR
GUEST OF GOD	DEIFALLAH	ضيفالله	DEIYF-AL-LAH
GUIDE	DALEEL	دليل	DAH-LEEL
GUIDE FOR MY LIFE	DAHLIL HAYATI	دليل حياتي	DAH-LEEL-HAH-YAH-TEE
GUIDED ONE	MEHDI	مهدي	MEH-DEE
GUN POWDER	BAROUD	بارود	BAH-ROOD
		– H –	
HALTER	RASAN	رسنة	RAH-SAHN
HAPPINESS	FARAH	فرح	FAH-RAH
HAPPINESS	MARAH	مرح	MAH-RAH
HAPPY, LIVELY, JUBILANT	FARHAN	فرحانة	FAHR-HAHN
HAVE THE UPPER HAND	MOUSSAYTER	مسيطر	MOO-SAY-TER
HEADGEAR	TARBOUSH	طربوش	TAHR-BOOSH
HEART	FOUAD	فؤاد	FOO-ADD
HEAVEN	SAMAH	سماح	SAH-MAH
HELLO, GREETING	MARHABA	مرحبة	MAR-HAH-BAH
HERMIT	NASEK	ناسك	NAH-SEK
HERO	BATTAL	بطل	BAH-TAHL
HIGH DEGREE OF EXCELLENCE, PERFECTION	KAMAL	كمال	KAH-MAHL
HIGH REGARD, RESPECT	WEEQAR	وقار	WEE-KAR
HIGHLY INTELLIGENT	NABIL	نبيل	NAH-BEEL
HOLY CAMPAIGN, RESISTANCE	JIHAD	جهاد	JEE-HAD
HOLY MAN	MOUFTI	مفتي	MOOF-TEE
HOLY MAN	SHEIK	شيخ	SHEEK

Mouhra (Filly)

ENGLISH	ARABIC		PRONUNCIATION
– G –			
GRAPEVINE	DALIAT	داليـة	DAH-LEE-YAHT
GRATEFUL	FADOOLIYAH	فاضولية	FAH-DOO-LEE-YAH
GRATEFUL	SHAKIRAH	شاكرة	SHAH-KEE-RAH
GRAY COLOR	SHABHAH	شبهة	SHAB-HAH
GREAT SIZE, LARGE, GIANT	KABIREH	كبيرة	KAH-BEE-REH
GREAT, MAGNIFICENT	JALEELAH	جليلة	JAH-LEE-LAH
GREETINGS, PEACE TO YOU	SALAMAT	سلامت	SAH-LAH-MAHT
GRIEVED	LAHFANEH	لهفانة	LAH-FAH-NEH
GROUNDS KEEPER, GUARD	NATOURAH	ناطورة	NAH-TOO-RAH
GUARD OF THE LIFE	HARISSEH AL HAYAT	حريسة الحياة	HAH-REE-SSEH-AL-HAH-YAHT
GUARDIAN OF MY HEART	NATOURAT ALBEE	ناطورة قلبي	NAH-TOO-RAHT-AHL-BEE
GUIDANCE, DIRECTION	NASIHAH	نصيحة	NAH-SEE-HAH
GUIDE	DALEELAH	دليلة	DAH-LEE-LAH
GUIDE FOR MY LIFE	DAHLILAT HAYATI	دليلة حياتي	DAH-LEE-LAHT-HAH-YAH-TEE
GUIDED	MEHDIEH	مهدية	MEH-DEE-YEH
GUN, RIFLE	BAROUDEH	بارودة	BAHR-ROO-DEH
– H –			
HAPPINESS	SAADAT	سعادات	SAH-AH-DAT
HAPPINESS ALWAYS	FARHANEH ALA TOOL	فرحانة على طول	FAHR-HAH-NEH-AH-LAH-TOOL
HAPPY ONE, LIVELY	FARHANEH	فرحانة	FAHR-HAH-NEH
HAVE THE UPPER HAND	MOUSSAYTIRAH	مسطيرة	MOO-SAY-TEE-RAH
HEADDRESS	KHUFFIYA	كفية	KHU-FEE-YAH
HEALTHY, WELL	SALEEMAH	سليمة	SAH-LEE-MAH
HEART BREAKER	KASSARAT AL QUALB	كسارة القلب	KAH-SAH-RAHT-AHL-QUAHLB

Mouher (Colt)

ENGLISH	ARABIC		PRONUNCIATION
		– H –	
HONEST, CLEAR	SARIH	صريح	SAH-REEH
HONEST, NOBLE, HONORABLE	SHARIF	شريف	SHAH-REEF
HONOR	SHARAF	شرف	SHAH-RAF
HOPE	AMAL	أمل	AH-MAHL
HORNET	ZANBOUR	زنبور	ZAN-BOOR
HORSE	FARAS	فرس	FAH-RAHS
HORSE OF BEST BREED	KAHIL	كحيل	KAH-HEEL
HORSEMAN	FAREES	فارس	FAH-REES
HORSEMAN	KHAYYAL	خيال	KHAY-YAHL
HORSEMAN FOR THE AGES	KHAYYAL ZAMAN	خيال زمانه	KHAY-YAHL-ZAH-MAN
HORSEMEN	FOURSAN	فرسانة	FOOR-SSAN
HORSERACER	JAWAD	جواد	JAH-WAHD
HOT TO THE TOUCH	HAMEE	حامي	HAH-MEE
HOTEL	FOONDOC	خندقه	FOON-DOC
HUM (FROM HUMMING)	WAZWAZA	وزوزة	WAHZ-WAH-ZAH
HUMAN	INSANEE	إنساني	IN-SAH-NEE
HUMOR	HAZAL	هزل	HAH-ZAHL
HUMOROUS	HAZZAL	هزّال	HAH-ZZAHL
HUNCHED BACK	AHDAB	أحدب	AH-DAHB
HUNTER	SAYADD	صياد	SAH-YAHD
		– I –	
ILLUMINATED	MOUNAWAR	منور	MOO-NAH-WAHR
ILLUSION	WAHM	وهم	WAH-HIM
ILLUSTRATION	TAFSEER	تفسير	TAF-SEER

152

Mouhra (Filly)

ENGLISH	ARABIC		PRONUNCIATION
		– H –	
HEAVEN	SAMAH	سماى	SAH-MAH
HEAVENLY	SAMAWEEYEH	سماوية	SAH-MAH-WEE-YEH
HELLO (SALUTATION), PEACE TO YOU	SALAMEH	سلامة	SAH-LAH-MEH
HELLO, GREETING	MARHABA	مرحبة	MAR-HAH-BAH
HEROINE	BATALEH	بطلة	BAH-TAH-LEH
HIGH DEGREE OF EXCELLENCE, PERFECTION	KAMAL	كمال	KAH-MAL
HIGH RANK	RIFAT	رفعة	REE-FAHT
HIGH REGARD, RESPECT	WEEQAR	وقار	WEE-KAHR
HIGHLY INTELLIGENT	NABILA	نبيلة	NAH-BEE-LAH
HILL, HEIGHT	RABWAT	ربوة	RAB-WAHT
HOLY CAMPAIGN, RESISTANCE	JIHAD	جهاد	JEE-HAD
HONEST, CLEAR	SARIHAH	صريحة	SAH-REE-HAH
HONOR	SHAHAMAT	شهامة	SHAH-HAH-MAT
HONOR	SHARAF	شرف	SHAH-RAF
HONORABLE, HONEST, NOBLE	SHARIFAH	شريفة	SHAH-REE-FAH
HOPE	AMAL	أمل	AH-MAHL
HORSERACER	JAWADEH	جوادة	JAH-WAH-DEH
HORSEWOMAN	KHAYYALEH	خيالة	KHAY-YAH-LEH
HOW BEAUTIFUL	MA AJMALA	ما اجملة	MAH-AJ-MAH-LAH
HUM (FROM HUMMING)	WAZWAZAH	وزوزة	WAZ-WAH-ZAH
HUMANITY, POLITENESS	INSANIAT	إنسانية	IN-SAH-NEE-YAHT
HUMOROUS	HAZZALEH	هزالة	HAH-ZAH-LEH
HUNCHED BACK	HADBAH	حدبة	HAHD-BAH
HUNTER	SAYADDAH	صيادة	SAH-YAH-DAH

Mouher (Colt)

ENGLISH	ARABIC		PRONUNCIATION
		– I –	
IMAGE	SOURAT	صورة	SOO-RAHT
IMAGINATION	KHATER	خاطر	KHAH-TER
IMMORTAL, FOREVER	DAYEM	دايم	DAH-YEM
IMPRISONED	SAJEEN	سجين	SAH-JEEN
IN LOVE	HAWI	هاوي	HAH-WEE
INFLUENTIAL, POWERFUL	QADIR	قدير	KAH-DEER
INGENIOUS	FAHIM	فهيم	FAH-HEEM
INHERITENCE	REZEK	رزقة	REH-ZEK
INSPECTOR	NAZER	ناظر	NAH-ZER
INSPIRED	MOWAHAB	موهب	MOO-WAH-HAB
INTEGRITY	KAHMAL	كمال	KAH-MAHL
INTELLIGENT	LABIB	لبيب	LAH-BEEB
INTELLIGENT, CLEVER	ZAKEE	زكي	ZAH-KEE
INTERMEDIARY	WASSIT	وسيط	WAH-SEET
INTIMATE	NADIM	نديم	NAH-DEEM
INTOXICATED	SAKRAN	سكرانة	SAHK-RAHN
INTRIGUE	DASSAHYES	دسايس	DAH-SAH-YISS
IRANIAN KING	SHAH	شاه	SHAH
IRON	HADDID	حديد	HAH-DEED
		– J –	
JEALOUSY, ENVY	HASSAD	حسد	HAH-SAD
JOKER	HAZZAR	هزّار	HAH-ZAHR
JONAH	YUNIS	يونس	YOO-NEES
JOURNEY	MOUSHWAR	مشوار	MOOSH-WAHR

154

Mouhra (Filly)

ENGLISH	ARABIC		PRONUNCIATION
		– I –	
IGNITION	ISHTIAAL	إشتعال	ISH-TEE-AAL
ILLUMINATED	MOUNAWARAH	منورة	MOO-NAH-WAH-RAH
IMMORAL	FASSEEDAH	فاسدة	FAH-SEE-DAH
IN DEMAND	MATLOOBEH	مطلوبة	MAHT-LOO-BEH
IN GOOD HEALTH	TAYYEB	طيب	TAH-YEB
IN LOVE	HAWIYAH	هاوية	HAH-WEE-YAH
IN THE MORNING	SABIHAH	صبيحة	SAH-BEE-HAH
INCOME	WARED	وارد	WAH-RED
INFLUENTIAL	QADIRAH	قديرة	KAH-DEE-RAH
INGENIOUS	FAHIMAH	فاهمة	FAH-HEE-MAH
INHERITENCE	REZKAH	رزقة	REHZ-KAH
INSPECTOR	NAZEERAH	نظيرة	NAH-ZEE-RAH
INSPIRATION	ELHAM	إلهام	EL-HAM
INSPIRATION	MAWAHEB	مواهب	MAH-WAH-HEB
INTEGRITY	KAHMAL	كمال	KAH-MAHL
INTELLIGENT, CLEVER	ZAKIEH	زكية	ZAH-KEE-YEH
INTERMEDIARY	WASSITAH	واسطة	WAH-SEE-TAH
INTIMATE	NADIMAH	نديمة	NAH-DEE-MAH
INTOXICATED	SAKRANEH	سكرانة	SAHK-RAH-NEH
ISLAND	JAZIRAH	جزيرة	JAH-ZEE-RAH
		– J –	
JASMINE	YASMIN	ياسمين	YAS-MEEN
JEALOUSY, ENVY	HASADDEH	حسادة	HAH-SAD-DEH
JEWEL, PEARL	JAWHARAT	جوهرة	JAHW-HAH-RAHT

155

Mouher (Colt)

ENGLISH	ARABIC		PRONUNCIATION
		– J –	
JOY, PLEASE	SURUR	سرور	SOU-ROO-R
JUDGE	KADI	قاضي	KAH-DEE
JULY	TAMOUZ	تموز	TAH-MOOZ
JUMPER	KHAFAZ	قفاز	KAH-FAHZ
JUVENILE	SABI	صبي	SAH-BEE
		– K –	
KEPT, ONE THAT YOU KEEP	MAHFOUZ	محفوظ	MAH-FOOZ
KICKER	RAFFAS	رفاس	RAH-FAHS
KIND, GOOD HEARTED, GENTLE	ANIS	أنيس	AH-NEES
KINDRED, RELATIVE	NASIB	نسيب	NAH-SEEB
KING OF AN EMIRATE	SULTAN	سلطان	SUL-TAHN
KING, RULER	MALIK	مالك	MA-LIK
KINGDOM, EMPIRE	MAMLAKEE	مملكة	MAM-LAH-KEE
KISS	KOUBLAH	قبلة	KOO-BLAH
KISS OF THE SHADOW	KOUBLAT AL ZILAL	قبلة الزلال	KOO-BLAHT-AHL-ZEE-LAHL
KURDISH ORIGIN	KURDI	كردي	KUHR-DEE
		– L –	
LANCER	RAMEH	رامح	RAH-MEH
LANTERN, LAMP	FANOUS	فانوس	FAH-NOOS
LARGE CUP	FINJAN KABEER	فنجان كبير	FEEN-JAHN-KAH-BEER
LARGE, GIANT	KABIR	كبير	KAH-BEER
LAZY	BALEED	بليد	BAH-LEED
LAZY	KASSLAN	كسلان	KAHSS-LAN
LAZY AND CONTENT	BALEED WE RADEE	بليد وراضي	BAH-LEED-WEH-RAH-DEE

Mouhra (Filly)

ENGLISH	ARABIC		PRONUNCIATION
– J –			
JOKER	HAZZARAH	حزّارة	HAH-ZAH-RAH
JOURNEY	MOUSHWAR	مشوار	MOOSH-WAHR
JOURNEY	RAHLAT	رحلة	RAH-LAHT
JUDGE	HAKEMEH	حاكمة	HAH-KEH-MEH
JUMPER	KHAFAZEH	قفازة	KAH-FAH-ZEH
JUVENILE	SABEEYAT	صبية	SAH-BEE-YAHT
JUVENILE	SABIYAH	صبية	SAH-BEE-YAH
– K –			
KICKER	RAFASSEH	رفاسة	RAH-FAH-SSEH
KIN, RELATIVE	NASIBAH	نسيبة	NAH-SEE-BAH
KIND AND ORPHANED	YATIMAH WAH HANOUNEH	يتيمة وحانونة	YAH-TEE-MAH-WAH-HAH-NOO-NEH
KIND, GENTLE, GOOD HEARTED	ANEESAH	أنيسة	AH-NEES-SAH
KINDNESS, GRACE	SAMAHAT	سماحة	SAH-MAH-HAHT
KINDRED	NASEEBAH	نسيبة	NAH-SEE-BAH
KISS	KOUBLAH	قبلة	KOU-BLAH
KISS OF THE SHADOW	KOUBLAT AL ZILAL	قبلة الزلال	KOO-BLAHT-AHL-ZEE-LAHL
KNOWLEDGE	DIRAYAT	دراية	DEER-AH-YAHT
KURDISH GIRL	KURDIEH	كردية	KUHR-DEE-YEH
KURDISH ORIGIN	KURDIYAH	كردية	KUHR-DEE-YAH
– L –			
LADY	SITT	ست	SITT
LAZY AND LOVED	KISLANEH WAH MAHBOUBEH	كسلانة ومحبوبة	KEES-LAH-NEH-WAH-MAH-BOO-BEH
LAZY, INACTIVE	BALEEDAH	بليدة	BAH-LEE-DAH
LEAD (METAL), BULLET	RASASSA	رصاصة	RAH-SAH-SSAH

Mouher (Colt)

– L –

ENGLISH	ARABIC	PRONUNCIATION
LEAD (METAL), BULLET	RASAS	رصاص	RAH-SAS
LEAD AROUND	TAWAFF	طوافه	TAH-WAF
LEADER	MOUDEER	مودير	MOO-DEER
LEADER, CHIEF	ZAIM	زعيم	ZAH-EEM
LEADER, HOLY MAN	IMAM	إمام	EE-MAM
LEASE, HIRE, RENT	EJAR	إجار	EH-JAHR
LIAR, UNTRUTHFUL	DAJJAN	دجانه	DAH-JAN
LID OF THE EYE, EYELID	TARAF AL EIN	طرفه العين	TAH-RAHF-AHL-EIN
LIGHT	NOUR	نور	NOOR
LIGHT OF THE EYES	NOUR AL OUYOUN	نور العيونه	NOOR-AHL-OU-YOON
LIGHT OF THE SOUL	NOOR AL NOUFOUS	نور النفوس	NOOR -AHL- NOO-FOOS
LIGHTNING, THUNDER	RAAD	رعد	RAH-EID
LIKES TO TOUCH	DASSDASS	ددسس	DAHS-DAHS
LION	ASSAD	أسد	AH-SSAHD
LOCKSMITH	QAFFAL	قفال	KAHF-FAHL
LONG LEGS	TAWIL	طويل	TAH-WEEL
LOST	TAYEH	تايح	TAH-YEH
LOST AND IN DEMAND	TAYEH WAH MATLOUB	تايح ومطلوب	TAH-YEH-WAH-MAT-LOOB
LOVE	HOUB	حب	HOOB
LOVE MY DARLING	HOUB YA HABIBI	حب ياحبيبي	HOOB-YAH-HAH-BEE-BEE
LOVE STRICKEN	HAYEM	هايم	HAH-YEM
LOVE, AFFECTION	WEEDAD	وداد	WEE-DAD
LOVE, AFFECTION	HIYAM	هيام	HEE-YAHM
LOVER, BELOVED	HABIB	حبيب	HAH-BEEB

Mouhra (Filly)

ENGLISH	ARABIC		PRONUNCIATION
		– L –	
LEADER	MOUDEERAH	مديرة	MOO-DEE-RAH
LEADER	ZAIMEH	زاعيمة	ZAH-EE-MEH
LEFT	YASSAR	يسار	YAH-SAHR
LEFT HANDED	YOUSRAH	يوسرة	YOUS-RAH
LEMON	LEYMOONEH	ليمونة	LEH-MOON-NEH
LIAR, UNTRUTHFUL	DAJJANEH	دجانة	DAH-JAN-NEH
LIBERATION, FREEDOM	TAHREER	تحرير	TAH-REER
LIGHT OF THE EYES	NOUR AL OYOUN	نورالعيون	NOOR-AH-OO-YOON
LILY, IRIS	ZANBUK	زنبوك	ZAN-BOOK
LIVE COAL	JAMRAT	جمرة	JAHM-RAHT
LOCKSMITH	QAFFALEH	قفالة	KAHF-FAH-LEH
LONG LEGGED, TALL	TAWILAH	طويلة	TAH-WEE-LAH
LONG TERM GUEST	NAZEELAH	نزيلة	NAH-ZEE-LAH
LOST	TAYIHAH	تايهة	TAH-YEE-HAH
LOVE	HAWAH	هوا	HAH-WAH
LOVE, AFFECTION	HIYAM	هيام	HEE-YAHM
LOVE, AFFECTION	WEEDAD	وداد	WEE-DAD
LOVED ONE	HABAYEB	حبايب	HAH-BAH-YEB
LOVING, AFFECTIONATE	MOUHIBAH	محبة	MOO-HEE-BAH
LUKEWARM	FATTEERAH	فاترة	FAH-TEE-RAH
		– M –	
MAGNIFICENT, BOSS	AZIMEH	عظيمة	AH-ZEE-MEH
MANY HELLOS (used in Arabic songs)	HAIHAT	حيهات	HAI-HAHT
MANY NIGHTS	LEILAT	ليلات	LEH-LAHT

159

Mouher (Colt)

ENGLISH	ARABIC		PRONUNCIATION
		– L –	
LOYAL, BEST FRIEND	AMIN	أمين	AH-MEEN
LUKEWARM	FAHTER	فاتر	FAH-TEHR
		– M –	
MAGIC	SIHR	سحر	SEEHR
MAGICIAN	SAHER	ساحر	SAH-HEHR
MAGNIFICENT, BOSS	AZIM	عظيم	AH-ZEEM
MAJESTIC	MOUAZAR	مؤازر	MOO-AH-ZAHR
MANUAL	YADAWEE	يداوي	YAH-DAH-WEE
MARBLE	MURMUR	رخم	MUHR-MUHR
MARKET	BAZAR	بزار	BAH-ZAHR
MARTYR	SHAHEED	شاهيد	SHAH-HEED
MEDIATOR	WASEET	وسيط	WAH-SEET
MERCHANT	TAJER	تاجر	TAH-JER
MESSENGER	RASOUL	رسول	RAH-SOOL
METAL, LEAD	BOULAD	بولاد	BOO-LAD
MILD	HALEEM	حليم	HAH-LEEM
MISCHIEVOUS YOUNSTER	TAHYESH	طايش	TAH-YESH
MIXED CROWD	LAFEEF	لفيف	LAH-FEEF
MONEY	DERHAM	درهم	DER-HAHM
MONK	RAHEB	راهب	RAH-HEB
MOON	AMAR	قمر	AH-MAHR
MOON	KAMAR	قمر	KAH-MAHR
MORNING	SABAH	صباح	SAH-BAH
MORNING PERSON	SUBHI	صبحي	SOUB-HEE

160

Mouhra (Filly)

ENGLISH	ARABIC		PRONUNCIATION
		– M –	
MARBLE	MURMUR	دمرم	MUHR-MUHR
MARE	FARASE	فرسة	FAHR-AHS-EH
MARTYR	SHAHEEDAH	شهيدة	SHAH-HEE-DAH
MAY	AYAR	أيار	AH-YAHR
MEADOW	RAWDAH	روضة	RAW-DAH
MEDIATOR	WASEETAH	وسيطة	WAH-SEE-TAH
MELODY	GHOUNIAT	غنية	GHOO-NEE-YAHT
MERCHANT	TAJEERAH	تاجرة	TAH-JEE-RAH
MESSENGER	RASOULEH	رسولة	RAH-SOU-LEH
MILD	HALIMAH	حليمة	HAH-LEE-MAH
MILLION	MALYOUN	مليونة	MAL-YOON
MINISTER, ADVISOR	WAZIRAH	وزيرة	WAS-ZEE-RAH
MIRAGE	SARAB	سراب	SAH-RAB
MIRROR	MERAYAT	مراية	MEE-RAH-YAHT
MISCHIEVIOUS YOUNSTER	TAYISHAH	طائشة	TAH-YEE-SHAH
MIST, THIN CLOUD	DABAB	الضباب	DAH-BAHB
MODE, MANNER, STYLE	TEERAZ	طراز	TEE-RAHZ
MOISTURE, DEW	NADA	ندا	NAH-DAH
MOON	HILAL	هلال	HEE-LAHL
MOON	KAMAR	قمر	KAH-MAHR
MORNING DEW	RHEEMAH	ريمة	RHEE-MAH
MORNING PERSON	SUBHIYAH	صبحية	SOUB-HEE-YAH
MORNINGS	SABAHAT	صباحة	SAH-BAH-HAHT
MOST TRUSTED FRIEND	AMINEH	أمينة	AH-MEEN-EH

161

Mouher (Colt)

ENGLISH	ARABIC		PRONUNCIATION
		– M –	
MOUNTAIN	JABAL	جبل	JAH-BAL
MOVE ABOUT, GO AROUND	DAHWAR	دوادد	DAH-WAHRR
MOVIE STAR, STAR OF THE SCREEN	NEGM AL SHASHA	نجم الشاشة	NEHGM-AHL-SHAH-SHAH
MUDDY	BALGAMI	بلغمي	BAHL-GAH-MEE
MUSK	MISK	مسك	MEESK
MY GUEST	DEIFI	ضيفي	DEIY-FEE
MY LIFE	YA HAYATI	يا حياتي	YAH-HAH-YAH-TEE
MY TURN	DAWREE	دوري	DAHW-REE
MYSTIC	SURRI	سري	SOOR-REE
		– N –	
NARRATOR	RAHWEE	راوية	RAH-WEE
NECESSARY	LAZEM	لازم	LAH-ZEM
NECESSITY	LUZOUM	لزوم	LUH-ZOOM
NECK CHAIN	KURDAN	كردنة	KUHR-DAHN
NEW MOON, CRESCENT	HILAL	هلال	HEE-LAHL
NEW ONE	JADEED	جديد	JAH-DEED
NEXT DOOR NEIGHBOR	MOUJAWER	موجاور	MOU-JAH-WER
NIGHT	LEIL	ليل	LAY-IL
NIGHTINGALE	BOULBOUL	بلبل	BOOL-BOOL
NIGHTLAMP	SIRAJ AL LEIL	سراج الليل	SEE-RAJ-AHL-LAYIL
NILE	NIL	نيل	NEEL
NINTH MONTH OF MOSLEM YEAR	RAMADAN	رمضان	RAH-MAH-DAHN
NOBLE, GLORIOUS	MAJEED	ماجيد	MAH-JEED
NOBLE, LIBERAL, GIVER	KAREEM	كريم	KAH-REEM

Mouhra (Filly)

ENGLISH	ARABIC		PRONUNCIATION
		– M –	
MOUTH BIT	SHAKIMAT	نشاكيمة	SHAH-KEE-MAHT
MUDDY	BALGAMIYAH	بلغامية	BAHL-GAH-MEE-YAH
MY GUEST	DIEFEE	ضيفي	DEIY-FEE
MY LIFE	YA HAYATI	يا حياتي	YAH-HAH-YAH-TEE
MY LOVE	HABIBI	حبيبي	HAH-BEE-BEE
MYSTIC	SURIAH	سرية	SOO-REE-YAH
		– N –	
NARRATOR	RAHWIYAH	راوية	RAH-WEE-YAH
NAUGHTY, MISBEHAVING GIRL	SHARIRAH	شريرة	SHAH-REE-RAH
NECESSITY	DAROURAT	ضرورة	DAH-ROO-RAHT
NEEDLE	EBRA	إبرة	EB-RAH
NEW IN LOVE	JADEEDAH BIL HOUB	جديدة بالحب	JAH-DEE-DAH-BIL-HOOB
NEW ONE	JADEEDEH	جديدة	JAH-DEE-DEH
NEXT DOOR NEIGHBOR	MOUJAWIRAH	مجاورة	MOU-JAH-WEE-RAH
NIGHT	LEILAH	ليلة	LEH-LAH
NOBLE, GLORIOUS	MAJEEDAH	ماجدة	MAH-JEE-DAH
NOBLE, LIBERAL	KARIMAH	كريمة	KAH-REE-MAH
NON-BELIEVER	KAHFIRAH	كافرة	KAH-FEE-RAH
NORTHERN OR NORTHERLY	SHEEMALI	شمالي	SHEE-MAH-LEE
NUN	RAHEBAH	راهبة	RAH-HEH-BAH
		– O –	
OBLIGATION	MAMNOONIEH	ممنونية	MAM-NOO-NEE-YIEH
OH, BEAUTIFUL ONE	YA JAMEELAH	يا جميلة	YAH-JAH-MEE-LAH

163

Mouher (Colt)

ENGLISH	ARABIC	PRONUNCIATION

– N –

| NON-BELIEVER | KAFER | كافِر | KAH-FER |
| NOTORIOUS | SHAHEER | شاهِير | SHAH-HEER |

– O –

OATH, TO THE RIGHT	YAMEEN	يمين	YAH-MEEN
OH, MOM	YA-OUMEE	يا اُمي	YAH-OU-MEE
OH, BEAUTIFUL ONE	YA JAMEEL	يا جميل	YAH-JAH-MEEL
OH, GOD	YA ALLAH	يا الله	YAH-ALLAH
OH, ZEID	YA ZEID	يا زيد	YAH-ZED
OLD ONE	AJOUZ	عجوز	AH-JOOZ
OLIVE	ZAITOON	زيتونة	ZAHY-TOON
ONE OF A KIND, RARE ONE	NADIR	نادِر	NAH-DEER
ONE OF A KIND, UNIQUE	FAREED	فريد	FAH-REED
ONE OF SIGNIFICANCE, FAMOUS	MOUSHTAHER	مشتهر	MOOSH-TAH-HEHR
ONE WHO FORGIVE	MOUSSAMEH	مسامح	MOO-SSAH-MEH
ONE WHO LEARNS, STUDENT	TELMIZ	تلميذ	TEL-MEEZ
ONE WHO OBJECTS	RAFED	رافض	RAH-FED
ONE WHO PLEADS A CAUSE	WAKEEL	وكيل	WAH-KEEL
ONE WHO STANDS BAIL	KAFIL	كفيل	KAH-FEEL
ONE-EYED	AAWAR	أعور	AAH-WAHR
ONLY CHILD	WAHEED	وحيد	WHAH-HEED
ONLY ONE, UNIQUE	WAHED	واحد	WHAH-HED
ORIGINAL	AWALEE	أولي	AH-WAH-LEE
ORNAMENT	ZEENAT	زينة	ZEE-NAHT
ORPHAN	YATIM	يتيم	YAH-TEEM

Mouhra (Filly)

ENGLISH	ARABIC		PRONUNCIATION
		– O –	
OH, DARLING	YA HABIBTEE	يا حبيبتي	YAH-HAH-BEEB-TEE
OH, DAUGHTER OF THE WIND	YA BINT AL RIYAH	يا بنت الرياح	YAH-BINT-AHL-REE-YAH
OLD ONE	AJOUZEH	عجوزة	AH-JOOZ-EH
OLIVES	ZAITUNAT	زيتونة	ZAHY-TOO-NAHT
ONCE UPON THE TIME	KAN YAMA KAN	كان يا مكان	KAHN-YAH-MAH-KAHN
ONE OF A KIND, RARE	NADIRAH	نديرة	NAH-DEE-RAH
ONE THAT YOU KEEP, KEPT	MAHFOUZAH	محفوظة	MAH-FOO-ZAH
ONE WHO FORGIVES	MOUSSAMEHAH	مسامحة	MOO-SSAH-MEH-HAH
ONE WHO LEARNS, STUDENT	TELMIZEH	تلميزة	TIL-MEE-ZEH
ONE WHO LIKES TO TOUCH	DASSDASSAH	دسدسة	DAHS-DAH-SAH
ONE WHO PLEADS A CAUSE	WAKEELAH	وكيلة	WAH-KEE-LAH
ONE-EYED	AWRAH	عورة	AHW-RAH
ONLY DAUGHTER	WAHEEDAH	وحيدة	WHAH-HEE-DAH
OPENING SHOW	FOURJAH	فرجة	FOOR-JAH
ORIENTAL DANCE	DABKEH	دبكة	DAHB-KEH
ORIGINAL	AWALIYAH	أولية	AH-WAH-LEE-YAH
ORNAMENT	ZEENAT	زينة	ZEE-NAHT
ORPHAN	YATEEMAH	يتيمة	YAH-TEE-MAH
ORPHAN	YATIMAH	يتيمة	YAH-TEE-MAH
OUTSIDER	BARRANIYAH	برانية	BAH-RAH-NEE-YAH
OVER GARMENT	FARJIYAH	فرجية	FAHR-JEE-YAH
OVERLY ACTIVE, ENERGETIC	IRDEH	إردة	IRR-DEH
OVERSIZED, BULKY	JAHSSIMAH	جسيمة	JAH-SEE-MAH
OWNER	MALEEKAH	مالكة	MAH-LEE-KAH

Mouher (Colt)

ENGLISH	ARABIC	PRONUNCIATION
– O –		
OUTSIDER	BARRANI	BAH-RAH-NEE
OVERLY INTELLIGENT AND CUNNING	ZAKI KTEER	ZAH-KEE-KTEER
OWNER	MAHLIK	MAH-LIK
OXEN YOKE, A MEASURE	FADDAN	FAHD-DAHN
– P –		
PAGEANT, FEAST, CONCERT	MAHRAJAN	MAH-RAH-JAHN
PAINTER	DAHHAN	DAH-HAN
PALATIAL	LAHAWEE	LAH-HAH-WEE
PANTHER, LYNX	FAHD	FAHD
PARADISE	FIRDOUSS	FIR-DOUSS
PARTNER	SHAREEK	SHAH-REEK
PASSION	HAYAHJAN	HAH-YAH-JAN
PASSIONATE	MOUHEB	MOO-HEB
PASSIVE	MAJHOOL	MAHJ-HOOL
PATIENCE (HAVING)	SABIR	SAH-BEER
PATIENT	SABR	SAHBER
PATRON	WALEE	WAH-LEE
PEACE	SALAM	SAH-LAHM
PEACE BE WITH YOU	SALAM MAAKOUM	SAH-LAHM-MAAH-KOUHM
PEACEFUL, SAFE	SALEEM	SAH-LEEM
PEACOCK	TAWOOS	TAH-WOOSS
PEANUTS	FOUSTOK	FOOS-TOC
PEARL	LULU	LOO-LOO

166

Mouhra (Filly)

ENGLISH	ARABIC		PRONUNCIATION

– P –

ENGLISH	ARABIC		PRONUNCIATION
PAINTER	DAHANEH	دحانة	DAH-HAH-NEH
PARADISE	FERDOUS	فردوس	FEHR-DOWS
PARTNER	SHAREEKAH	شريكة	SHAH-REE-KAH
PASSIONATE	MOUHEBAH	محبة	MOO-HEH-BAH
PASSIONATE LOVE	HEHYAM	هيام	HEH-YAHM
PASSIVE	MAJHOOLAH	مجهولة	MAJ-HOO-LAH
PATIENCE (TO HAVE)	SABIRAH	صابرة	SAH-BEE-RAH
PATRON	WALEEYAT	وليت	WAH-LEE-YAHT
PAUSE IN TIME	BOURHAH	برها	BOOR-HAH
PEACEFUL, SAFE	SALIMEH	سليمة	SAH-LEE-MEH
PEARL	LOULOU	لولو	LOO-LOO
PEARL	LULU	لولو	LOO-LOO
PENITENT	NAHDEEMAH	نديمة	NAH-DEE-MAH
PEPPER (TREE OR FRUIT)	FULFUL	فلفل	FULL-FULL
PERFECTION, WITHOUT FAULT	FAHDEELAH	فاظلة	FAH-DEE-LAH
PHILOSOPHER	FAYLASSOOFAH	فيلسوفة	FAY-LAH-SOU-FAH
PHYSICIAN	TABIBAH	طبيبة	TAH-BEE-BAH
PICTURE, FORM	SOURAT	صورة	SOO-RAHT
PILOT	TAYYAR	طيار	TAH-YAHR
PLANE	TAYYARAH	طيارة	TAH-YAH-RAH
PLEASANT	BAHEEJAH	باهجة	BAH-HEE-JAH
PLEDGE	RAHEENAT	راهنة	RAH-HEE-NAHT
POEM, SONG	NASHEEDAT	نشيدات	NAH-SHEE-DAHT
POLITE	ADIBEH	أديبة	AH-DEE-BEH

Mouher (Colt)

ENGLISH	ARABIC		PRONUNCIATION
		– P –	
PENITENT	NADEM	ناحم	NAH-DEM
PEOPLE OF	BANI	باني	BAH-NEE
PERFECTION IN BEAUTY	KAMAL AL HOUSN	كمال الحسنة	KAH-MAHL-AHL-HOOSN
PERFECTION, WITHOUT FAULT	FADEL	فاضل	FAH-DELL
PERPETUAL LIAR	DAJJAL ALA TOOL	دجال علا طول	DAH-JAHL-AH-LAH-TOOL
PERSON WHO LIVES NEAR SEA	SHATAWEE	شنطاوي	SHAH-TAH-WEE
PHILOSOPHER	FAYLASSOOF	فيلاسوفه	FAY-LAH-SSOOF
PHYSICIAN	TABIB	طبيب	TAH-BEEB
PILGRIMAGE TO MECCA	HAJJ	حج	HAJJ
PILOT	TAYYAR	طيار	TAH-YAHR
PIN	DABBOUS	دبوس	DAHB-BOOS
PINE TAR	KOUTRAN	قطرانه	KOO-TRAN
PIPER	ZAMMAR	زمار	ZAH-MAR
PLEASANT	BAHIJ	بهيجي	BAH-HEEJ
PLENTIFUL	ZAYID	زايد	ZAH-YEED
POLITE	ADIB	أديب	AH-DEEB
POPULAR SON	IBN SHAABEE	إبنه شعبي	IBN-SHAA-BEE
PORCH, HALL	EWAN	إوانه	EE-WAHN
PORT IN ISRAEL	EILAT	إيلات	EE-LAHT
POSTMASTER	RAHS AL BOOSTA	راس البوسطة	RAHS-AHL-BOOS-TAH
PRAISE BE TO GOD	HAMDALLAH	حمدلله	HAM-DAH-LAH
PRAISE BE TO GOD	SOUBHAN ALLAH	صبحانه الله	SOOB-HAN-AHL-LAH
PRAISED	MAMDOOH	ممدوح	MAM-DOOH
PREACHER	KHOURY	خوري	KHOU-REE

Mouhra (Filly)

ENGLISH	ARABIC		PRONUNCIATION
		– P –	
POSSESSED, OWNED	MAMELUKAH	محلوكة	MAH-MEH-LOO-KAH
PRAISED	MAMDOOHAH	ممدوحة	MAM-DOO-HAH
PREACHER	KHOURYEH	خورية	KHOO-REE-YEH
PRECIOUS GEM	FAREEDAH	فريدة	FAH-REE-DAH
PRECIOUS OBJECT	KARIMEH	كريمة	KAH-REE-MEH
PRECIOUS STONE	JAWAHER	جواهر	JAH-WAH-HEHR
PRESENT WORLD	DOUNIAH	دنية	DOO-NEE-AH
PRESENTATION	TAKDIMAH	تقديمة	TAHK-DEE-MAH
PRETTY ONE	HELWETT	حلوة	HEL-WETT
PRETTY, BEAUTIFUL	GAMILAH	جميلة	GAH-MEEL-AH
PREY	FARESSAH	فارسة	FAHR-ESS-AH
PRINCESS	AMIRAH	أميرة	AH-MEER-AH
PRINCESS	EMEERA	أميرة	EH-MEE-RAH
PRINCESS	EMIRA	أميرة	EH-MEE-RAH
PRINCESS	WAJEEHAH	وجيهة	WHAH-JEE-HAH
PRINCESS OF THE COLORS	AMIRAT AL ALWAN	أميرة الألوان	AH-MEER-AHT-AL-AHL-WAHN
PRISONER	ASIRA	أسيرة	AH-SEE-RAH
PRISONER	MASJOUNEH	مسجونة	MAHS-JOO-NEH
PRISONER	SAJEENA	سجينة	SAH-JEE-NAH
PRISONER OF MY LIFE	SAJINAH HAYATI	سجينة حياتي	SAH-JEE-NAH-HAH-YAH-TEE
PRIVILEDGE	MOUTAMAYEZAH	متمايزة	MOO-TAH-MAH-YEH-ZAH
PRIZE, PRESENT	JAWAIZ	جوائز	JAH-WAH-EZ
PROMINENT	BARIZAH	بارزة	BAH-REE-ZAH
PROPHETIC	NABAWIAH	نباوية	NAH-BAH-WEE-YAH

169

Mouher (Colt)

ENGLISH	ARABIC		PRONUNCIATION
		– P –	
PRESENTATION	TAKDEEM	تقديم	TAHK-DEEM
PRETTY ONE	HELOU	حلو	HEH-LOO
PRETTY, BEAUTIFUL	GAMIL	جميل	GAH-MEEL
PRINCE	EMEER	أمير	EH-MEER
PRINCE	EMIR	إمير	EH-MEER
PRINCE, KING	AMIR	أمير	AH-MEER
PRISONER	ASSEER	أسير	AH-SEER
PRISONER	MASJOUN	مسجونة	MAHS-JOON
PRISONER OF MY HEART	SAJIN ALBEE	سجين قلبي	SAH-JEEN-AL-BEE
PRISONER OF MY LIFE	SAJIN HAYATI	سجين حياتي	SAH-JEEN-HAH-YAH-TEE
PRIVILEDGE	MOUTAMAYEZ	موتمايز	MOO-TAH-MAH-YEZ
PRIZE	MUJAZAT	مجزاة	MOO-JAH-ZAHT
PROMINENT	BARIZ	بارز	BAH-REEZ
PROPHETIC	NABAWEE	نبوي	NAH-BAH-WEE
PROSPEROUS	YASIR	يسر	YAH-SEER
PROTECTED ONE (BY GOD)	MAHROUSS	محروس	MAH-ROOSS
PROTECTOR	HARESS	حارس	HAH-RESS
PROTECTOR OF THE HOUSE	HARESS AL DAR	حارس الدار	HAH-RESS-AHL-DAHR
PROTECTOR, GUARDIAN	HAMI	حامي	HAH-MEE
PROUD	FAHKOUR	فاخور	FAH-KOOR
PRUDENT, RESOLUTE	HAZEM	حازم	HAH-ZEM
PUPIL (OF THE EYE)	BASSBOUSS	بسبوس	BAHSS-BOOSS
PURE	ASIL	عسيل	AH-SEEL
PURE GOLD	EBRIZ	إبريز	EB-RIZ

Mouhra (Filly)

ENGLISH	ARABIC		PRONUNCIATION
	– P –		
PROSPEROUS	YASIRAH	يا سرة	YAH-SEE-RAH
PROTECTED	MEHMIYEH	محمية	MEH-MEE-YEH
PROTECTED ONE (BY GOD)	MAHROUSSEH	محروسة	MAH-ROO-SSEH
PROTECTION	HIMAYAT	حماية	HEE-MAH-YAHT
PROTECTOR	HARISSAH	حارسة	HAH-REE-SSAH
PROUD	FAKOURAH	فاخورة	FAH-KOO-RAH
PUPIL (OF THE EYE)	BASSBOUSSAH	بسبوسة	BASS-BOO-SSAH
PUPIL, STUDENT	TALEEBAT	طالبة	TAH-LEE-BAHT
PURE	ASILEH	عسيل	AH-SEE-LEH
PURE BRED, BEST BREED	KAHILEH	كاحيلة	KAH-HEE-LEH
PURE, CLEAN	NAHZEEFAH	نظيفة	NAH-ZEE-FAH
PURE, VIRGIN	TAHEERAH	طاهرة	TAH-HEE-RAH
PURITY	TAHARAT	طاهرات	TAH-HAH-RAHT
	– Q –		
QUANTITY	KAMIYAT	كمية	KAH-MEE-YAHT
QUEEN OF AN EMIRATE	SULTANAH	سلطانة	SUL-TAH-NAH
QUEEN, RULER	MALIKAH	مالكة	MA-LEE-KAH
QUIET, LAID BACK	BASEETAH	بسيطة	BAH-SEE-TAH
QUIZ, TEST	HAZZOURAH	هزورة	HAH-ZOO-RAH
	– R –		
RAGING	HAYEJAH	هايجة	HAH-YEH-JAH
RECENT, NEW	JADEEDAH	جديدة	JAH-DEE-DAH
RED FLOWER	ZAHRAH HAMRAH	زهرة حمراء	ZAH-RAH-HAM-RAH
RED ROSE	WARDI HAMRAH	وردي حمراء	WAHR-DEE-HAM-RAH

Mouher (Colt)

ENGLISH	ARABIC		PRONUNCIATION
		– P –	
PURE, CLEAN	NAHZEEF	ناضيفة	NAH-ZEEF
PURE, CLEAN	TAHER	طاهر	TAH-HER
PYRAMID	AHRAM	أهرام	AH-RAHM
		– Q –	
QUEST	TALAB	طلب	TAH-LAHB
QUIET	HADEE	هادي	HAH-DEE
		– R –	
RAGING	HAYEJ	هايج	HAH-YEHJ
RAIN	MATTAR	مطر	MAH-TAHR
REBELLIOUS	MARID	مارد	MAH-REED
REDEEMER	FADEE	فادي	FAH-DEE
REJECTED	MARFOUD	مرفوض	MAHR-FOOD
REJOICING	FERHAN	فرحانة	FEHR-HAHN
RELIABLE	WASSIK	واثقة	WAH-SEEK
RELIEF	FARAJ	فرج	FAH-RAHJ
RELIGION	DEEN	دينة	DEEN
RESPECT, HIGH ESTEEM	IHTERAM	إهترام	IH-TEE-RAM
REVENGE	TAR	طار	TAHR
REVERSAL, CHANGE OF MIND	TAKLIB	تقليب	TAHK-LEEB
RIVAL	MOUNAFES	مناقس	MOO-NAH-FESS
RIVER	NAHR	نهر	NAHER
ROAD	SABEEL	سبيل	SAH-BEEL
ROAD	TARIK	طريق	TAH-REEK

Mouhra (Filly)

ENGLISH	ARABIC		PRONUNCIATION
		– R –	
REFINEMENT	LATAFAT	لطافة	LAH-TAH-FAHT
REGRET, REPENTENCE	NADAMAT	ندامة	NAH-DAH-MAHT
REJECTED	MARFOUDAH	مرفوضة	MAHR-FOO-DAH
REJOICING	FERHANEH	فرحانة	FEHR-HAHN-EH
RELIABLE	WASSIKAH	واثقة	WAH-SEE-KAH
RENOWNED	MOUSHTAHIRAH	مشتهرة	MOOSH-TAH-HEE-RAH
REPENTENCE	TAWBAT	توبة	TAW-BAHT
REPUBLIC	JAMHOURIAT	جمهورية	JAM-HOO-REE-YAHT
RESPECT, HIGH ESTEEM	IHTERAM	إحترام	IH-TEE-RAM
RESTED	MERTAHAH	مرتاحة	MER-TAH-HAH
REVERENCE, MODESTY	HISHMAT	هشمة	HISH-MAHT
REVERSAL, CHANGE OF MIND	TAKLIBAH	تقليبة	TAHK-LEE-BAH
RIGHT SIDE	YUMNAT	يمنة	YOOM-NAHT
ROAD	TAREEK	طريق	TAH-REEK
ROAMING, LOST	SHAREEDAH	شريدة	SHAH-REE-DAH
ROMANCER	RAWIYAH	راوية	RAH-WEE-YAH
ROPE, CORD	MARSAT	مرساة	MAHR-SAHT
ROSE COLORED	WARDI	وردي	WAHR-DEE
ROSES	WOUROUD	ورود	WOO-ROOD
RUMBLING, TO SHAKE	ZALZALEH	زلزلة	ZAL-ZAH-LEH
		– S –	
SAFE, FREE FROM DANGER	SALIMAH	سليمة	SAH-LEE-MAH
SALESWOMAN	SEMSARAH	سمسارة	SEM-SAH-RAH
SASSY	MALOUNEH	ملعونة	MAH-LOO-NEH

173

Mouher (Colt)

ENGLISH	ARABIC		PRONUNCIATION
		– R –	
ROAD COMPANION	MORAFIC	وافقة	MOO-RAH-FEK
ROAMING	SHARED	شارد	SHAH-RED
ROCKING (OF WAVES, ETC)	HADEER	هدير	HAH-DEER
ROPE DANCER	BAHLAWAN	بهلوانة	BAH-LAH-WAHN
ROPE MAKER, TWISTER	FATTAL	فتال	FAHT-TAHL
RUBY	YAKOUT	ياقوتة	YAH-KOOT
RULE, REGULATION	DASTOUR	دستور	DAHS-TOOR
		– S –	
SAFE, PEACEFUL	SALIM	سالم	SAH-LEEM
SALESMAN	SEMSAR	سمسار	SEM-SAHR
SAND	RAML	رمل	RAH-MEL
SANDSTORM	KAMSEEN	خمسين	KAHM-SEEN
SASSY	MALOUN	ملعونة	MAHL-OON
SATISFACTION	REDWAN	رضوانة	RED-WON
SCARED, FRIGHTENED	FAZAAN	فزعانة	FAHZ-AHN
SCEPTOR	SAWLAJAN	صولجانة	SAW-LAH-JAN
SEEKER, SEARCHING FOR SOMETHING	MOUFATESH	مفتش	MOO-FAH-TESH
SENSUAL, PASSIONATE	SHAHWAN	شهوانة	SHAH-WAN
SESAME SEED	SOMSOUM	سمسم	SOOM-SOOM
SEVENTH MONTH OF MOSLEM YEAR	RAJAB	رجب	RAH-JAB
SHADOW	ZILAL	زلال	ZEE-LAHL
SHADOW OF LOVE	ZILAL AL HAWAH	زلال الهوا	ZEE-LAHL-AHL-HAH-WAH
SHARP SWORD	HUSSAM	حسام	HUH-SSAM

Mouhra (Filly)

ENGLISH	ARABIC		PRONUNCIATION
		– S –	
SAVED BY THE GRACE OF GOD	SALIMAH MIN ALLAH	سالمة من الله	SAH-LEE-MAH-MIN-AHL-LAH
SCAR	NADBAT	ندبة	NAHD-BAT
SCARED	FAZAANEH	فزعانة	FAHZ-AAH-NEH
SCHEDULE	LAYEHAT	لائحة	LAH-YEH-HAHT
SECRET THOUGHT	DAMEER	ضمير	DAH-MEER
SECURITY, BAIL	KAFALEH	كفالة	KAH-FAH-LEH
SEEKER, SEARCHING FOR SOMETHING	MOUFATESHAH	مفتشة	MOO-FAH-TESH-AH
SENSUAL, PASSIONATE	SHAHWANEH	شهوانة	SHAH-WAH-NEH
SEPARATION, FLIGHT	HIJRAT	هجرة	HEEJ-RAHT
SEPTEMBER	AYLOUL	أيلول	AY-LOOL
SESAME SEED	SOUMSOUM	سمسم	SOOM-SOOM
SESSION, GATHERING	JALSAT	جلسة	JAHL-SAHT
SET OF SAME KIND	WAJBAT	وجبة	WAHJ-BAT
SHADOW	ZILAL	زلال	ZEE-LAHL
SHADOW OF LOVE	ZILAL AL HAWAH	زلال الهوا	ZEE-LAHL-AHL HAH-WAH
SHADOW OF MY HEART	ZILAL ALBEE	زلال قلبي	ZEE-LAHL-AHL-BEE
SHINING, BEAUTIFUL	BAHIEH	بهية	BAH-HEE-YEH
SHOCK	SADMAT	صدمة	SAHD-MAHT
SIGN	ISHARAT	إشارات	E-SHAH-RAHT
SIGNIFICANT, FAMOUS	MOUSHTAHERAH	مشهرة	MOOSH-TAH-HEHR-AH
SILK BROCADE	DIBAJEH	ديباجه	DEE-BAH-JEH
SILVER	FIDDAT	فضة	FEED-DAHT
SIMPLE	BAHSEETAH	بسيطة	BAH-SEE-TAH
SIMPLE AND BEAUTIFUL	BALADIEH WAH HELWEH	بلدية وحلوة	BAH-LAH-DEE-YEH-WAH-HEL-WEH

175

Mouher (Colt)

ENGLISH	ARABIC		PRONUNCIATION
		– S –	
SHOPKEEPER	DOUKANJEE	دكانجى	DOO-KAHN-JEE
SIGN	ISHARAT	إشارة	E-SHAH-RAHT
SILK BROCADE	DIBAJ	ديباج	DEE-BAHJ
SIMPLE AND BEAUTIFUL	BALADI WE HELOU	بلدى وحلو	BAH-LAH-DEE-WEH-HEH-LOO
SIMPLE, QUIET, LAID BACK	BASEET	بسيط	BAH-SEET
SINGULAR	FARDANI	فردانى	FAHR-DAH-NEE
SKILLFUL	MAHER	ماهر	MAH-HER
SLIM, SLENDER	RASHEEK	رشيقه	RAH-SHEEK
SLY	DAHI	داهى	DAH-HEE
SMALL BELL	JULJUL	جلجل	JOOL-JOOL
SMALL QUANTITY	TAFIF	طفيفه	TAH-FEEF
SNAKE	HANASH	حنش	HAH-NASH
SNOW	TALJ	ثلج	TAHLJ
SO AND SO	KAZA WAH KAZA	كزا وكزا	KAH-ZAH-WAH-KAH-ZAH
SOFT	LAYYIN	لَيّنه	LAH-YEN
SOFT BREEZE	NASEEM	نسيم	NAH-SEEM
SOLDIER	JUNDEE	جنده	JUN-DEE
SON OF THE PEACE	IBN AL SALAM	إبنه السلم	IBN-AHL-SAH-LAHM
SON OF THE NILE	IBN AL NIL	إبنه النيل	IBN-AHL-NEEL
SON OF THE WIND	IBN AL RIYAH	إبنه الرياح	IBN-AHL-REE-YAH
SONG	NASHEED	نشيد	NAH-SHEED
SOUND MAKER	RANNAN	رنانه	RAH-NAN
SPECIAL ONE, LOVED ONE	MAHBOUB	محبوب	MAH-BOUB
SPECIAL, UNIQUE	NADER	نادر	NAH-DER

Mouhra (Filly)

ENGLISH	ARABIC		PRONUNCIATION
		– S –	
SINGULAR	FARDANIYAH	مردانية	FAHR-DAH-NEE-YAH
SKILLFUL	MAHEERAH	ماهرة	MAH-HEE-RAH
SLAP ON THE FACE	LATMAH	لطمة	LAHT-MAH
SLAVE GIRL	JARIYAT	جارية	JAH-REE-YAHT
SLENDER, ELEGANT FORM	RASHEEKAH	رشيقة	RAH-SHEE-KAH
SLUGGISH, LAZY	KASSLANEH	كسلانة	KAHSS-LAH-NEH
SLY	DAHIYAH	داهية	DAH-HEE-YAH
SMALL CUP, TEA CUP	FINJAN	فنجانة	FIN-JAHN
SMALL PIECE	FARMAT	حرمت	FAHR-MAHT
SMART, ALERT	FAHEEMEH	فهيمة	FAH-HEE-MEH
SMART, INTELLIGENT	LABIBAH	لبيبة	LAH-BEE-BAH
SO AND SO	KAZA WAH KAZA	كزا او كزا	KAH-ZAH-WAH-KAH-ZAH
SOCIABLE, FRIENDLY	ANISAH	أنيسة	AH-NEES-SAH
SOFT	LAYYENAH	لينة	LAH-YEH-NAH
SOFT HEARTED	HANOUNEH	حنونة	HAH-NOO-NEH
SOFT SPOKEN, QUIET	SAKEETAH	ساكتة	SAH-KEE-TAH
SOFTNESS	LOUYOUNEH	ليونة	LOUH-YOO-NEH
SOLID	JAMIDAT	جامدة	JAH-MEE-DAHT
SORREL COLOR	SHAKRAH	شقرة	SHAHK-RAH
SOUL OF THE HEART	NOUFOUS	نفوس	NOO-FOOS
SOUL, LIFE	MOUHJAT	موهجة	MOO-JAHT
SOUND MAKER	RAHNANAH	رنانة	RAH-NAH-NAH
SOUND OF WIND	ZAFEER	زفير	ZAH-FEER
SOUTHERNER	JENOUBEE	جنوبي	JEH-NOO-BEE

Mouher (Colt)

ENGLISH	ARABIC		PRONUNCIATION
		– S –	
SPIRIT, SOUL	NOUFOUS	نفوس	NOO-FOOS
SPLENDOR, MAJESTY	JALAL	جلال	JAH-LAHL
SPOILED, BAD	FASSED	فاسد	FAH-SSED
SPONGE	ISPHANJ	إسفنج	ISS-FANJ
SPRING (SEASON)	RABI	ربيع	RAH-BEE
SPUNKY, LIVELY, CRAZY	MAJNOUN	مجنونة	MAHJ-NOON
SPY	DASSOUS	داسوس	DAH-SOOS
STALLION	FAHL	فحل	FAH-HELL
STAR	NEGM	نجم	NEHGM
STAR IN THE SKY	KAWKAB	كوكب	KAW-KAHB
STEEL	FOULAZ	فولاذ	FOO-LAHZ
STIFF, FIRM	JAHMED	جامد	JAH-MED
STIPULATION, CONDITION	SHART	شرط	SHAHRT
STONE	HAJAR	حجر	HAH-JAR
STRANGER	GHARIB	غريب	GAH-REEB
STREET	SABIL	سبيل	SAH-BEEL
STREET	TAREEK	طريقة	TAH-REEK
STREET OF LOVE	SABIL AL HAWAH	سبيل الهوا	SAH-BEEL-AHL-HAH-WAH
STRONG BELIEF	YAKIN	يا قين	YAH-KEEN
STRONG ONE, WARRIOR	ANTAR	عنتر	AHN-TAR
STRONG, PROUD	JABBAR	جبار	JAH-BAHR
STUBBORN	ANID	عنيد	AH-NEED
STUDENT, SEEKER OF KNOWLEDGE	TALEB	طالب	TAH-LEB
SUBSTITUTE	BADAL	بدل	BAH-DAHL

Mouhra (Filly)

ENGLISH	ARABIC		PRONUNCIATION
		– S –	
SPARK	SHARARAT	ثرارة	SHAR-RAH-RAHT
SPECIAL ONE, LOVED ONE	MAHBOUBEH	محبوبة	MAH-BOO-BEH
SPECIAL, UNIQUE	NADEERAH	نادرة	NAH-DEE-RAH
SPEECHLESS	KAZEM	خازم	KAH-ZEM
SPIRAL	LOWLABEE	لولبي	LOW-LAH-BEE
SPIRITUAL	ROUHANI	روحاني	ROU-HAH-NEE
SPLENDOR, MAJESTY	JALALAT	جلالة	JAH-LAH-LAHT
SPONGE	ISPHANJE	إسفنجي	ISS-FAN-JEH
SPUNKY, LIVELY, CRAZY	MAJNOUNEH	مجنونة	MAHJ-NOO-NEH
SPY	DASSOUSSEH	دسوسة	DAH-SOOS-SEH
STAR	NEGM	نجم	NEHGM
STAR (IN THE SKY)	KAWKABEH	كوكبة	KAW-KAH-BEH
STARS	KAWAKEB	كواكب	KAH-WAH-KEB
STERILE, BARE	JADBAH	جدبة	JAHD-BAH
STIFF, FIRM	JAHMIDAH	جامدة	JAH-MEE-DAH
STIPULATIONS, CONDITIONS	SHURUT	شروط	SHOO-ROOT
STORM	ASSEEFAH	عاصفة	AHS-SEE-FAH
STORY, TALE	HIKAYAT	حكايات	HEE-KAH-YAHT
STRANGER	GHARIBEH	غريبة	GHA-REE-BEH
STRONG, MUSCULAR	SHADEEDEH	شديدة	SHAH-DEE-DEH
STRONG, PROUD	JABBARAH	جبارة	JAH-BAH-RAH
STUBBORN	ANIDEH	عنيدة	AH-NEED-EH
STUDENT, SEEKER OF KNOWLEDGE	TALIBAH	طالبة	TAH-LEE-BAH
SUCCESS	NAJIHAH	ناجحة	NAH-JEE-HAH

Mouher (Colt)

ENGLISH	ARABIC		PRONUNCIATION
		– S –	
SUCCESS	NAJAH	نجاح	NAH-JAH
SUN	SHAMS	شمس	SHAHMS
SURGEON	JARRAH	جراح	JAH-RAH
SURPRISED	MUHTAR	مختار	MUH-TAHR
SUSPECT	SHABEEH	شبيه	SHAH-BEAH
SUSPICION	SHAKK	نشك	SHAHK
SWAGGERER (CONCEITED STRUT)	FASHAR	فشار	FAH-SHAR
SWEET, PLEASANT	LAZIZ	لذيذ	LAH-ZEEZ
SWINDLER, THIEF	NASSAB	نصاب	NAH-SAB
SWORD	SEIF	سيفه	SAYF
		– T –	
TALL	TAWEEL	طويل	TAH-WEEL
TAME	DAJIN	داجين	DAH-JEEN
TARGET, AIM, GOAL	HADAF	هدفه	HAH-DAHF
TEARFUL	BAKI	باكى	BAH-KEE
TEMPERAMENT	MIZAJ	مزاج	MEE-ZAHJ
TEMPLE	HAIKAL	هيكل	HAI-KAHL
TENDER	NAHIF	نحيفه	NAH-HEEF
TESTIFIERS, WITNESSES	SHOUHUUD	شهود	SHOO-HOOD
THANK YOU	SHOUKRAN	نشكرا	SHOUK-RAHN
THANKFUL	SHAKUR	شاكر	SHAH-KOOR
THE APPLE OF THE EYES	AMAL AL OYOUN	أمل العيونه	AH-MAHL-AHL—OU-YOUN
THE AUTUMN OF MY LIFE	KHARIF AL OUMR	خريفه العمر	KHAH-REEF-AHL-OUMR

180

Mouhra (Filly)

ENGLISH	ARABIC		PRONUNCIATION

– S –

ENGLISH	ARABIC		PRONUNCIATION
SUFFICIENT	KIFAYA	كفاية	KEE-FAH-YAH
SUMMER	SAIFEEYEH	صيفية	SAHY-FEE-YEH
SUN	SHAMS	شمس	SHAHMS
SUPERIOR	ALEEYAH	عالية	AH-LEE-YAH
SURPRISED	MUHTARAH	محتارة	MUH-TAH-RAH
SUSPECT	SHABEEHAH	شبيهة	SHA-BEE-HAH
SUSPICION	SHOUKOUK	شكوك	SHOO-KOOK
SWAGGERER (CONCEITED STRUT)	FASHARAH	فشارة	FAH-SHAH-RAH
SWEET, PLEASANT	LAZIZA	لذيذة	LAH-ZEE-ZAH
SWEETNESS	HALAWA	حلاوة	HAH-LAH-WAH
SWINDLER, THIEF	NASABEH	نصابة	NAH-SAH-BEH

– T –

ENGLISH	ARABIC		PRONUNCIATION
TALISMAN, CHARM	TALSAM	طلسم	TAL-SAM
TALL, LONG LEGGED	TAWILEH	طويلة	TAH-WEE-LEH
TAME	DAJINAH	داجنة	DAH-JEE-NAH
TASSEL	SHARRABAT	شرابة	SHAH-RAH-BAHT
TEAR	DAMAA	دمعة	DAHM-MAH
TEARFUL	BAKIYAH	باكية	BAH-KEE-YAH
TENDER TO THE TOUCH, LEAN	NAHIFAH	نحيفة	NAH-HEE-FAH
TENT	KAIMAT	خيمة	KAY-MAHT
TESTIFIERS, WITNESSES	SHOUHUUD	شهود	SHOO-HOOD
THANKFUL	SHAKURA	شاكرة	SHAH-KOO-RAH
THE ARAB MARE	AL ARABIA	العربية	AHL-AR-RAH-BEE-YAH
THE BELOVED THIEF	NASABEH WAH MAHBOUBEH	نصابة ومحبوبة	NAH-SAH-BEH-WAH-MAH-BOO-BEH

Mouher (Colt)

ENGLISH	ARABIC		PRONUNCIATION
		– T –	
THE BLUISH-GREY ONE	EL AZRAK	ألأزرقه	EL-AHZ-RAHK
THE BRIDGE OF LOVE	JISR AL HAWAH	جسر الهوا	JISER-AL-HAH-WAH
THE BULKY CHESTED ONE	JASEEM AL SADR	جسيم الصدر	JAH-SEEM-AHL-SADR
THE CLEAR EYED ONE	SAFI AL OUYOUN	صافي العيون	SAH-FEE-AHL-OU-YOON
THE COLD HEARTED ONE	BARED AL NAHFS	بارد النفس	BAH-RED-AHL-NAHFS
THE COUNTRY	AL WATTAN	الوطنه	AHL WHAH TAHN
THE COURT OF A HOUSE	AL DAR	الدار	AHL-DAHR
THE COURTHOUSE	EL SARAYA	السرايا	EL-SAH-RAH-YAH
THE DELIGHTFUL COLORS	LAZEEZ AL ALWAN	لزيز الالوانة	LAH-ZEEZ-AHL-AHL-WAHN
THE DESERT HORSEMEN	FOURSAN AL SAHRA	فرسانه الصحرا	FOOR-SSAN-AHL-SAH-RAH
THE DESERT STAR	NEGM AL SAHRAH	نجم الصحراء	NEHGM-AHL-SAH-RAH
THE FIELD	AL MARJ	المرج	AHL-MAHRJ
THE FIVE	AL KHAMSAH	أخمسة	AHL-KHAHM-SAH
THE FIVE ONES	AL KHAMSEH	أخمسة	AHL-KAHM-SEH
THE FOUNTAIN OF LOVE	NAWAFIR AL HAWAH	نوافير الهوا	NAH-WAH-FEER-AHL-HAH-WAH
THE GIFT	AL HADIYEH	الهدية	AHL-HAH-DEE-YEH
THE GOAL	AL HADAF	الهدفه	AHL-HAH-DAHF
THE GOOD HEARTED SOUL	TAYYEB AL NAFS	طيب النفس	TAH-YEB-AHL-NAHFS
THE GRAY	AL SHAYIB	الشايب	AHL-SHAH-YEEB
THE GREAT ONE	AL KABEER	الكبير	AHL-KAH-BEER
THE HEART BREAKER	KASSAR AL ALB	كسر القلب	KAH-SSAR-AHL-AHLB
THE HERO	AL BATAL	ابطال	AHL-BAH-TAHL
THE HIGH EAGLE	NISR AL AALEE	نسر العالي	NEESR-AHL-AH-LEE
THE HOUSE OF PEACE	DAR EL SALAM	دار السلوم	DAR-EL-SAH-LAHM

Mouhra (Filly)

ENGLISH	ARABIC		PRONUNCIATION
		– T –	
THE BLUISH-GRAY ONE	AL ZARKA	الزرقاء	AHL-ZAHR-KAH
THE CITY OF PEACE, BAGDAD	MADINAT AL SALAM	مدينة السلام	MAH-DEE-NAT-AHL-SAH-LAHM
THE COLD HEARTED ONE	BAREDAT AL NAFS	باردة النفس	BAH-REE-DAHT-AHL-NAHFS
THE DARLING OF MY LIFE	AZEEZAT HAYATI	عزيزة حياتي	AH-ZEE-ZAHT-HAH-YAH-TEE
THE DOOR OF HEAVEN	BAB EL SAMAH	باب السماء	BAWB-EL-SAH-MAH
THE FIVE ONES	AL KHAMSE	الخمسة	AHL-KAHM-SEH
THE FRIEND FOR LIFE	ZAMILEH AL OUMR	زميلة العمر	ZAH-MEE-LAH-AHL-OUMR
THE GARDEN	AL RABIAH	الرابية	AHL-RAH-BEE-YAH
THE GIFT	AL HADIYEH	الهدية	AHL-HAH-DEE-YEH
THE GOOD HEARTED SOUL	TAYEEBAH AL NAFS	طيبة النفس	TAH-YEE-BAH-AHL-NAHFS
THE GREAT ONE	AL KABEERAH	الكبيرة	AHL-KAH-BEE-RAH
THE GREY ONE	AL SHABHAH	الشبهة	AHL-SHAB-HAH
THE HOPE OF MY LIFE	AMAL HAYATI	أمل حياتي	AH-MAHL-HAH-YAH-TEE
THE HOPE OF THE ARAB	AMAL AL ARAB	أمل العرب	AH-MAHL-AHL-AH-RAHB
THE HOPE OF THE EYES	AMAL AL OYOUN	أمل العيون	AH-MAHL-AHL-OU-YOON
THE HUNCHBACK	AL HADBAH	الحدباء	AHL-HAHD-BAH
THE LIGHT OF THE SOUL	NOOR AL NOUFOUS	نور النفوس	NOOR-AHL-NOO-FOOS
THE MARK OF BEAUTY	AL SHAMAH	الشامة	AHL-SHAH-MAH
THE MORNING DEW OF MY LIFE	RHEEMAT HAYATEE	ريمة حياتي	RHEE-MAHT-HAH-YAH-TEE
THE NOBLE ONE	AL SHARIFAH	الشريفة	AHL-SHAH-REEF-AH
THE OLD ONE	EL AJOUZ	العجوز	EL-AH-JOOZ
THE ONE EYED MARE OR FILLY	EL AWRAH	العوراء	EL-OUW-RAH
THE ONE OF RARE BEAUTY	NADIRAH AL JAMEELAH	نديرة الجميلة	NAH-DEE-RAH-AHL-JAH-MEE-LAH
THE PERFECT DESCRIPTION	KAMELAT AL AWSAF	كاملة الأوصاف	KAH-MEE-LAHT-AHL-AHW-SAHF

Mouher (Colt)

ENGLISH	ARABIC		PRONUNCIATION
		-T -	
THE LIGHT OF MY LIFE	NOUR HAYATI	نور حياتي	NOOR-HAH-YAH-TEE
THE MOUNTAIN	AL JABAL	الجبل	AHL-JAH-BAL
THE NILE	EL NIL	النيل	EL-NEEL
THE NOBLE ONE	AL SHARIF	الشريف	AHL-SHAH-REEF
THE ONE-EYED COLT	EL AAWAR	الاعور	EL-AH-WAHR
THE ONLY ONE (ALLAH)	AL WAHEED	الوحيد	AHL-WHAH-HEED
THE PALACE	AL QUASR	القصر	AHL-QUASR
THE PERFECT DESCRIPTION	KAMEL AL AWSAF	كامل الاوصافه	KAH-MEL-AHL-AHW-SAHF
THE PRETTY EYED ONE	GAMIL AL OYOUN	جميل العيونه	GAH-MEEL-AHL-OU-YOON
THE PRETTY THIEF	NASSAB AL JAMEEL	نصاب جميل	NAH-SAB-AHL-JAH-MEEL
THE PROTECTED ONE	EL MAHROUSS	المحروس	EL-MAH-ROOSS
THE PURE SOUL, THE CLEAN SOUL	TAHER AL NAFS	طاهر النفس	TAH-HER-AHL-NAHFS
THE RARE BEAUTY	NADER AL JAMAL	نادر الجمان	NAH-DER-AHL-JAH-MAHL
THE RED ONE, THE BAY	AL AHMAR	الاهمي	AHL-AH-MAHR
THE REDEEMER	AL FADEE	الفادي	AHL-FAH-DEE
THE ROAD	AL SABIL	السبيل	AHL-SAH-BEEL
THE SHORE OF ARABIA	SHAT AL ARAB	شط العرب	SHAHT-AHL-ARAB
THE SOUTH WIND	EL MAREES	الماريس	EL-MAHR-REES
THE SPY	AL JASSOUS	الجاسوس	AHL-JAH-SOOS
THE STREET OF LOVE	TAREEK AL HAWAH	طريقة الهوا	TAH-REEK-AL-HAH-WAH
THE WELL-KNOWN ONE	AL MAAROUFF	المعروفه	AHL-MAH-ROOF
THE WING OF LOVE	JEENAH AL HAWAH	جناح الهوا	JEE-NAH-AHL-HAH-WAH
THE WISH OF MY LIFE	AMAL HAYATI	أمل حياتي	AH-MAHL-HAH-YAH-TEE
THE YELLOW	AL ASFAR	الاصفر	AHL-AHS-FAHR

Mouhra (Filly)

ENGLISH	ARABIC		PRONUNCIATION
		-T-	
THE PROTECTED ONE	AL MAHROUSSE	المحروسة	AHL-MAH-ROO-SSEH
THE PURE ONE	AL SAFIAT	الصافية	AHL-SAH-FEE-YAHT
THE PURE SOUL, THE CLEAN SOUL	TAHIRAH AL NAFS	طهرة النفس	TAH-HEE-RAH-AHL-NAHFS
THE RED ONE, THE BAY	AL HAMRAH	الحمراء	AHL-HAHM-RAH
THE SHINING ONE	AL BAHIEH	البهية	AHL-BAH-HEE-YEH
THE SOUL	AL NEFOUS	النفوس	AHL-NOU-FOOS
THE SPY	AL JASSOUSSAH	الجاسوسة	AHL-JAH-SOO-SSAH
THE STAR OF THE SCREEN, MOVIE STAR	NEGMAH AL SHASHA	نجمة الشاشة	NEHG-MAH-AHL-SHAH-SHAH
THE TANNED ONE	AL SAMRAH	السمرة	AHL-SAHM-RAH
THE TOWN	AL MADINAH	المدينة	AHL-MAH-DEE-NAH
THE TRAVELER OF THE COUNTRY	DAWARAT AL BEELAD	دوارة البلد	DAH-WAHR-AHT-AHL-BEE-LAHD
THE WHITE HOUSE	DAR AL BAIDAH	دار البيضة	DAHR-AHL-BAY-DAH
THE WHITE PEARL	LULU AL ABYAD	لؤلؤ الأبيض	LOO-LOO-AHL-AHB-YAHD
THE WING OF LOVE	JEENAH AL HAWAH	جناح الهوا	JEE-NAH-AHL-HAW-WAH
THE WORD	AL KELMAT	الكلمة	AHL-KEL-MAHT
THE YELLOW ONE	AL SAFNAH	الصفنة	AHL-SAHF-NAH
THIEF	HARAMIYEH	حرامية	HAH-RAH-MEE-YEH
THIEF	NAHHABEH	نهابة	NAH-HAH-BEH
THROW	RAMYAT	رامية	RAHM-YAHT
THROWER	RAHMIYAH	رامية	RAH-MEE-YAH
TIGRESS	NEMRAH	نمرة	NEM-RAH
TIME	ZAMAN	زمان	ZAH-MAN
TO BE GRIEVED	HAZINEH	حزينة	HAH-ZEE-NEH
TO BE INFATUATED WITH	LAHHABEH	لهابة	LAH-HAH-BEH

185

Mouher (Colt)

ENGLISH	ARABIC		PRONUNCIATION
		– T –	
THEOLOGIAN	LAHOOTEE	لاهوتة	LAH-HOO-TEE
THIEF, SWINDLER	NAHHAB	نهاب	NAH-HAB
THIMBLE	KISHTABAN	كشتبانة	KISH-TAH-BAHN
THROWER	RAHMEE	رامي	RAH-MEE
TIGER	NIMR	نمر	NIMR
TIME, AGE	DAHR	دهر	DAHR
TIMES, AGES	DOUHOUR	دهور	DOO-HOOR
TIP	BAKSHEESH	بخشيش	BAHK-SHEESH
TO BE OWNED	MAMELUK	مملوكة	MAH-MEH-LOOK
TO BEND	LAWWA	لوا	LAH-WAH
TO CONFIDE A SECRET TO	NAJEE	ناجي	NAH-JEE
TO FEAR	WAJAL	وجل	WHAH-JAHL
TO GATHER (AS A GROUP)	LAMLAM	لملم	LAHM-LAHM
TO HOPE	RAJA	رجاء	RAH-JAH
TO RETURN	EYAB	إياب	EE-YAHB
TO SHAKE, RUMBLING	ZALZAL	زلزال	ZAL-ZAL
TO TOUCH	LAMEES	لامس	LAH-MEES
TOMORROW	BOUKRA	بكرا	BOO-KRAH
TOWER	BIRJ	برج	BURJ
TOWER	BURJ	برج	BOORJ
TOWN IN SAUDI ARABIA	TAIF	طائفة	TAH-IF
TRANSLATOR	MOUTARJEM	مترجم	MOO-TAHR-JEHM
TRANSLATOR	TOURJUMAN	ترجمانة	TOOR-JOO-MAN
TRANSPARENT	SHAFFAHF	شفافة	SHAH-FAHF

186

Mouhra (Filly)

ENGLISH	ARABIC		PRONUNCIATION
		– T –	
TO BE SPOILED	DALAL	دلال	DAH-LAHL
TO COMMIT A CRIME	JENAYAT	جنايه	JEH-NAH-YAHT
TO STAY WITH ME FOREVER	DAYIMAH WAYAYAH	دايمة وايايا	DAH-YEE-MAH-WAH-YAH-YAH
TONE OF VOICE	LAHJAT	لهجة	LAH-JAHT
TOWER	BURJ	برج	BOORJ
TRANSLATOR	TOURJAMANEH	ترجمانة	TOOR-JAH-MAH-NEH
TRANSPARENT	SHAFFAFEH	شفافة	SHAH-FAH-FEH
TRAVELER	MOUSAFEERAH	مسافرة	MOO-SAH-FEE-RAH
TRAVELER, WANDERER	DAWARAH	دوارة	DAH-WAHR-AH
TREMBLING	RAJFAT	رجفة	RAJ-FAHT
TRIBULATION	SHADAHYED	شدايد	SHAH-DAH-YED
TRIUMPHANT	MOUFTAKERAH	مفتخرة	MOOF-TAH-KEH-RAH
TROUBLE MAKER	MISHKALJIYAH	مشكلجية	MISH-KHAHL-JEE-YAH
TRUE FRIEND FOR LIFE	SADEEKAT AL HAYAT	صديقة الحياة	SAH-DEE-KAHT-AHL-HAH-YAT
TRUE FRIENDSHIP	SADAKAT	صداقات	SAH-DAH-KAHT
TRUSTWORTHY FRIEND	AMEENAH	أمينة	AH-MEE-NAH
TRUTHFUL	SADIKAH	صادقة	SAH-DEE-KAH
TURKISH WOMAN	TURKIYEH	تركية	TUR-KEE-YEH
TURQUOISE	FAYROUZ	فيروز	FAY-ROOZ
TWINKLING OF AN EYE	TARFAT	طرفات	TAR-FAHT
		– U –	
UNDERSTANDING	FITNAT	فطنة	FIT-NAHT
UNION, SOLITUDE	WEHDAT	وحدة	WEH-DAHT
UNITED UNION	ITTIHAD	إتحاد	IT-TEE-HAD

Mouher (Colt)

ENGLISH	ARABIC		PRONUNCIATION
		– T –	
TRAVELER	MOUSAFER	مسافر	MOO-SAH-FER
TRIBULATION	SHADAT	شدة	SHAH-DAT
TRIUMPHANT	MOUFTAKER	مفتخر	MOOF-TAH-KEHR
TROUBLE	MASHAKEL	مشاكل	MAH-SHAH-KEL
TROUBLE MAKER	MISHKALJEE	مشكلجي	MISH-KAHL-JEE
TROUBLE, CALAMITY	DAHIYAT	داهية	DAH-HEE-YAHT
TRUE FRIEND	SADEEK	صديق	SAH-DEEK
TRUSTWORTHY	AMEEN	أمين	AH-MEEN
TRUTHFUL	SADEK	صادقة	SAH-DEK
TURK	TURKI	تركي	TUR-KEE
TWANG (SOUND MAKING)	RANEEN	رنين	RAH-NEEN
		– U –	
UNKNOWING, NOT KNOWING BETTER	JAHEL	جاهل	JAH-HEL
UPROAR	ZAJAL	زرجان	ZAH-JAL
USEFUL	FAYED	فايد	FAH-YED
		– V –	
VALLEY	WADI	وادي	WAH-DEE
VARIATION	EKTILAF	إختلافه	ICK-TEE-LAHF
VEIL, PARTITION	HIJAB	حجاب	HEE-JAHB
VENGEANCE	INTIKAM	إنتقام	IN-TEE-KAHM
VICTORY	NASR	نصر	NAHSR
VIGILANT, WATCHFUL	HARIS	حارس	HAH-REES
VINE	DAHWALEE	دوالي	DAH-WAH-LEE

Mouhra (Filly)

ENGLISH	ARABIC	PRONUNCIATION
– U –		
UNKNOWING, NOT KNOWING BETTER	JAHILAH	جاهلة	JAH-HEE-LAH
USEFUL	FAYEEDAH	فايدة	FAH-YEE-DAH
– V –		
VEIL WORN BY A WOMAN	SITAR	ستار	SEE-TAR
VEIL WORN BY A WOMAN	TARHAH	طرحة	TAR-HAH
VEILED	MOUHAJABEH	محجبة	MOO-HAH-JAH-BEH
VERY HAPPY	MARAH	مرح	MAH-RAH
VERY INTELLIGENT, SMART	FAHIMEH	فهيمة	FAH-HEE-MEH
VINE	DALEEYAT	دالية	DAH-LEE-YAHT
VIOLET	BANAFSAJI	بنفسجي	BAH-NAHF-SAH-GEE
VIRGIN	AZRAH	عزراء	AHZ-RAH
VIRTUE, EXCELLENCE	FADILAT	فاضيلة	FAH-DEE-LAHT
VISITING GUEST	ZAIRAH	زائرة	ZAH-YEAR-AH
VISITING MY HEART	ZAIRAHT ALBEE	زائرة قلبي	ZAH-YEAR-AHT-AHL-BEE
VISITOR	ZAYIRAH	زائرة	ZAH-YEE-RAH
VISITS	ZIYARAT	زيارات	ZEE-YAH-RAHT
VIVID	BAHIYAH	بهية	BAH-HEE-YAH
VIVIDNESS	ZAHAWAT	زهاوة	ZAH-HAH-WAHT
VOLCANO	BURKAN	بركان	BOUR-KAHN
– W –		
WAGER	REEHAN	رهان	REE-HAN
WAITING, EXPECTATION	INTIZAR	انتظار	IN-TEE-ZAR
WALKING	MASHEEYAH	ماشية	MAH-SHEE-YAH
WANTED, IN DEMAND	MATLOUBEH	مطلوبة	MAHT-LOU-BEH

Mouher (Colt)

ENGLISH	ARABIC		PRONUNCIATION
		– W –	
VIOLENT, STRONG	SHADEED	دشديد	SHAH-DEED
VISITOR	ZAYER	زائر	ZAH-YER
VISITS	ZIYARAT	زيارة	ZEE-YAH-RAHT
VIVID	BAHI	باهي	BAH-HEE
VIVIDNESS	ZAHAWAT	زهاوة	ZAH-HAH-WAHT
VOLCANO	BURKAN	بركانه	BOUR-KAHN
WAGER	REEHAN	ريحانه	REE-HAN
WAITING, EXPECTATION	INTIZAR	انتظار	IN-TEE-ZAR
WALKING	MASHEE	مشي	MAH-SHEE
WALL, ENCLOSURE	JEEDAR	جدار	JEE-DAHR
WANDERER, TRAVELER	DAWAR	دوار	DAH-WAHR
WANTED	MATLOUB	مطلوب	MAHT-LOOB
WASP	DAHBOOR	دابير	DAH-BOOR
WATER JET	NAFOURAH	نافورة	NAH-FOOR-AH
WEEK (7 DAYS)	JUMAA	جمعة	JUHM-AAH
WEEPER, LAMENTER	NADEB	نادب	NAH-DEB
WELCOME, OH WELCOME	HALA YA HALA	هلا يا هلا	HAH-LAH-YAH-HAH-LAH
WELL BEHAVED	ADEEB	أديب	AH-DEEB
WELL KNOWN	MAAROUF	معروفه	MAH-ROOF
WELL-OFF	MOUTAYASSIR	موتيسر	MOO-TAH-YAH-SER
WEST	GHARB	غرب	GHA-ERB
WHEEL	DOOLAB	دولاب	DOO-LAHB
WHERE ARE YOU PRETTY ONE	WAYNAK YA HELOU	وينك يا هلو	WAY-NAHK-YAH-HEH-LOO
WHERE ARE YOU?	WAYNAK	وينك	WAY-NAHK

190

Mouhra (Filly)

ENGLISH	ARABIC		PRONUNCIATION
		– W –	
WASP	DABOORAH	دابورة	DAH-BOO-RAH
WATER FOUNTAIN	NOWFARAT	نوفرة	NOW-FAH-RAHT
WATER PIPE	NARGILEH	نرجيلة	NAHR-JEE-LEH
WATERJET	NAHFOORAH	نافورة	NAH-FOO-RAH
WEARINESS	MALALAT	ملالات	MAH-LAH-LAHT
WEEPER, LAMENTER	NADIBAH	نادبة	NAH-DEE-BAH
WEIGHT	WAZNAT	وزنة	WAHZ-NAHT
WELCOME, OH WELCOME	HALA YA HALA	هلا يا هلا	HAH-LAH-YAH-HAH-LAH
WELL BEHAVED	ADEEBAH	أديبة	AH-DEE-BAH
WELL KNOWN	MAAROUFAH	معروفة	MAH-ROO-FAH
WELL-OFF	MOUTAYASIRAH	موتيسرة	MOO-TAH-YAH-SEE-RAH
WERE IT NOT FOR	LAWMA	لوما	LAW-MAH
WHERE ARE YOU PRETTY ONE?	WAYNEK YA HELWAH	وينك يا حلوة	WAY-NEK-YAH-HEL-WAH
WHERE ARE YOU?	INTE FEIN	انتي فين	IN-TEE-FEIN
WHERE ARE YOU?	WAYNEK	وينك	WAY-NEK
WHERE?	ELA EIN	ء اراينه	EELAH-EIN
WHISPER	HAMSAT	همسة	HAHM-SAHT
WHITE	BAYDAH	بيضة	BAHY-DAH
WHITE TIGRESS	NIMRAH BAIDAH	نمرة بيضة	NEEM-RAH-BAHY-DAH
WHITE, SO WHITE	BAIDAH SHU BAIDAH	بيضة شو بيضة	BAHY-DAH-SHOO-BAHY-DAH
WICKED ONE	FAJEERAH	فاجرة	FAH-JEER-AH
WICKED, DEVILISH	SHERIRAH	شريرة	SHEH-REER-RAH
WIDELY KNOWN	MASHOURAH	مشهورة	MASH-HOO-RAH
WIDOW	ARMALEH	أرملة	AR-MAH-LEH

Mouher (Colt)

ENGLISH	ARABIC		PRONUNCIATION
		– W –	
WHISPER	HAMSAT	همسة	HAHM-SAHT
WHITE	ABYAD	أبيض	AHB-YAHD
WHITE FALCON	SHAHEEN	شاهين	SHAH-HEEN
WHITE TIGER	NIMR ABYAD	نمر أبيض	NIMR-AHB-YAHD
WHY?	LEEMAZA	ليماذا	LEE-MAH-ZAH
WICKED ONE	FAJIR	فاجر	FAH-JEER
WICKED, DEVILISH	SHEREER	شرير	SHEH-REER
WIND	RIYAH	رياح	REE-YAH
WING	JEENAH	جناح	JEE-NAH
WINTERY	SHATAWI	شتاوي	SHAH-TAH-WEE
WISE	HAKEEM	حكيم	HAH-KEEM
WITTY, CLEVER, CUNNING	ZAKI	زكي	ZAH-KEE
WOLF	DEEB	ديب	DEEB
WOODCARVER	NADDAF	نداف	NAH-DAF
WOODCUTTER	HATTAB	حطاب	HAHT-TAB
WORDLY	DINYAWEE	دنياوي	DIN-YAH-WEE
WORKMAN, GUARD	HARRIS	حارس	HAH-REES
WORSHIPPER	SAJEED	سجيد	SAH-JEED
WRITER	KAHTEB	كاتب	KAH-TEB
		– Y –	
YOUNG MALE	SHABAB	شباب	SHAH-BAHB
YOUR MAJESTY	JALALAT	جلالة	JAH-LAH-LAHT
YOUR NAME IS?	ESMAK	إسمك	ISS-MAC
YOUR SHARE	NASSIBAK	نصيبك	NAS-SEE-BAK

Mouhra (Filly)

ENGLISH	ARABIC		PRONUNCIATION
		– W –	
WILL, TESTAMENT	WASSIYAH	وصية	WAH-SEE-YAH
WIND	RIYAH	رياح	REE-YAH
WING	JEENAH	جناح	JEE-NAH
WINTERY	SHATAWIYAH	شتاوية	SHAH-TAH-WEE-YAH
WISE	HAKIMEH	حكيمة	HAH-KEE-MEH
WISH	MONIET	منية	MOO-NIET
WISH OF THE SOUL	MONIET AL NEFOUS	منية النفوس	MOO-NIET-AHL-NOO-FOOS
WITTY, RESOURCEFUL	ZAKEEYEH	زكية	ZAH-KEE-YEH
WOLF	DEEBAH	ديبة	DEE-BAH
WOMAN OF A HOUSEHOLD	HAREEM	حريم	HAH-REEM
WOOD CUTTER	HATTABEH	حطابة	HAH-TAH-BEH
WORK, CRAFT	SANNAT	صنعة	SAHN-AHT
WORLD	DUNYAH	دنية	DOON-YAH
WORLDLY	DINYAWIYAH	دينياوية	DIN-YAH-WEE-YAH
WORSHIPPER	SAJIDAH	ساجدة	SAH-JEE-DAH
WRITER	KAHTEEBAH	كاتبة	KAH-TEE-BAH
		– Y –	
YELLOW	SAFRAH	صفراء	SAHF-RAH
YOUNG AT HEART, TEENAGER	JAHEELAH	جاهلة	JAH-HEE-LAH
YOUNG GIRL, YOUNG DAUGHTER	BINT SABIYEH	بنت صبية	BINT-SAH-BEE-YEH
YOUNG WOMAN	SABIYEH	صبية	SAH-BEE-YEH
YOUNG, YOUTHFUL	SABWAT	صبوات	SAB-WAHT
YOUR NAME IS?	ESMAKEE	إسمك	ISS-MAH-KEE

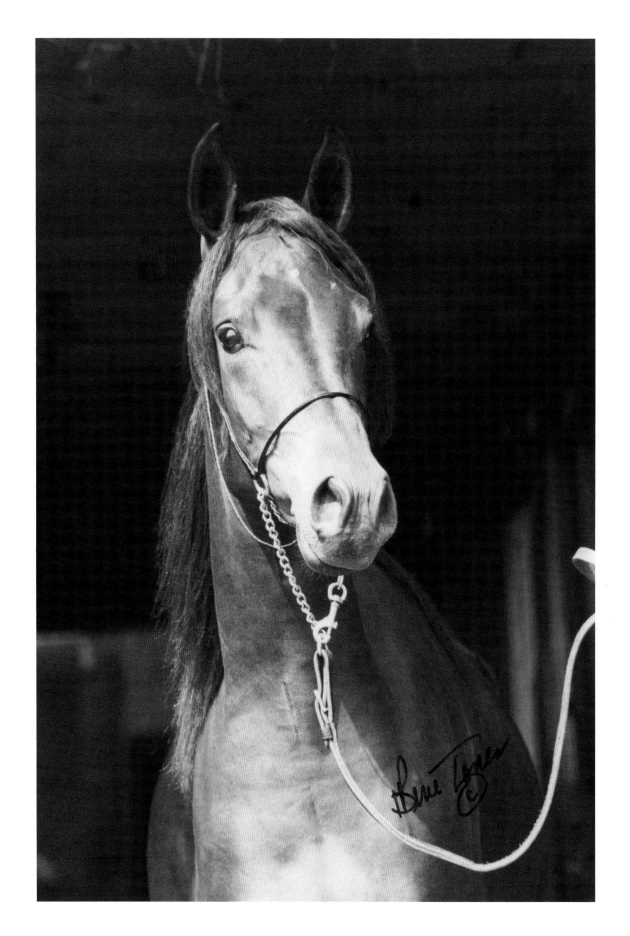

Sources of Additional Information about the Arabian Horse and its Middle Eastern Origin

ORGANIZATIONS

Al Khamsa, Inc.   7275 Manchester Rd., Capron, Illinois 61012.
Phone: 815-737-8102   Website: www.alkhamsa.org
A not-for-profit organization that seeks to preserve the bloodlines of Arabian horses, primarily in North America, who have descended entirely from the horses of the desert Bedouin tribes in the Middle East.

Arabian Horse Association   10805 East Bethany Drive., Aurora, Colorado 80014-2605.
Phone: 303-696-4500   Website: www.arabianhorses.org
A membership organization and official breed registry for Arabian, Half-Arabian, and Anglo-Arabian horses. Dedicated to preserving the integrity of and promoting the breed.

Asil Club   Hagentorwall 7, 31134 Hildesheim, Germany.
Phone. +49-(0)5121/150 10   Website: www.asilclub.de
An international membership association dedicated to the preservation of the rare Asil Arabian Horse, as bred by the Bedouin tribes of the Arabian peninsula and the Middle East. *Asil,* pronounced *ah-seel,* is an Arabic word meaning *pure.*

The Pyramid Society   P.O. Box 11941, Lexington, Kentucky 40579.
Phone: 859-231-6166 or 859-231-0771   Website www.PyramidSociety.org
An organization dedicated to the preservation of Straight Egyptian Arabian horses, whose bloodlines trace back solely to the deserts of Egypt and Arabia, and to the promotion of Egyptian bloodlines as an out cross.

PUBLICATIONS

The Classic Arabian Horse, by Judith Forbis. Published 1976.
A detailed history of the Arabian horse from ancient times to present day. Includes chapters on the horses of the Pharaoh's, Arabian horses in poetry, as well as information regarding Arabian horse strains. Also, includes a chapter on the Dancing Horses of the Nile Valley. Illustrated with photos, drawings, and artwork throughout the book.*

The Abbas Pasha Manuscript and Horses and Horsemen of Arabia and Egypt During the Times of Abbas Pasha, 1800-1860 by Judith Forbis and Gulsun Sherif. Published 1993.
A very thorough, historical account of the origins of the Arabian horse. Chronicles the Arabian's ancestry through horses acquired by Viceroy Abbas Pasha I of Egypt during the early 19th Century. Depicted are the Bedouin tribes of Arabia who fought to defend their Arabians, as well as the stud farms that were subsequently established abroad in Egypt and Europe. The Manuscript, included within this four book volume, is written from the Bedouin tribesmen's own words, as documented by the emissaries of Abbas Pasha. Filled with numerous art illustrations, plus many informative maps and charts.*

*The Classic Arabian Horse and The Abbas Pasha Munuscript available through:
Ansata Publications, 234 Polk 130, Mena, Arkansas 71953. Phone 479-394-5288. Website: www.ansata.com

Picture Credits

We would like to give a special acknowledgment to
award winning photographer, Irene Tones*, for the many beautiful
photographs which she provided and gave permission for
publication in this book. Irene has been capturing the
romance and beauty of the Arabian horse,
through her photography, for nearly 30 years.
Her captivating photos are very popular, especially
with Arabian horse owners and enthusiasts, and appear regularly in
nationally and internationally recognized Arabian horse publications and equestrian media.

Page	Credit
2	Courtesy of Rapture Arabians, ©Irene Tones
6	Abmor Acres collection
9	Kellie Kolodziejczyk
10-12	Bachir Bserani collection
13 *(top)*	Bachir Bserani collection
13 *(bottom)*	Joseph Crane
14	©Joe Ferriss
16	Kellie Kolodziejczyk
20	Kellie Kolodziejczyk
28	Bachir Bserani collection
30	Kellie Kolodziejczyk
32	Irene Tones
40	Irene Tones
42	Irene Tones
50	Courtesy of Rapture Arabians, ©Irene Tones
52	©Joe Ferriss
54	Provided by Abmor Acres, ©Irene Tones
124	Irene Tones
194	Courtesy of Rapture Arabians, ©Irene Tones
196	Irene Tones
198	Kellie Kolodziejczyk
200	Bachir Bserani collection

---

*Irene Tones Photography 1166 Old Talking Rock Highway, Talking Rock, GA 30175.
(706) 253-1478   Web site: www.iwtenterprises.com

And God
spoke,
"Bedouins,
let your
horses run
freely. . .and
you will be
rewarded
on
judgement
day."

In loving memory of
Don Diablo,
our family's magical and beloved
Arabian horse who peacefully
passed away during the production
of this book.

Bachir Bserani